THE ANIMATED CHILDREN'S KOSHER HOLIDAY COOKBOOK

Edited by:

**Yaacov Peterseil
Rivka Demsky**

Design and Graphics:

Barbara Citroen

Published by:

Ohr Torah Institutions
POB 1037
Efrat, Israel 90962

Distributed by:

Simcha Publishing Company
POB 101
Woodmere, New York, 11598

Ohr Torah Institutions gratefully acknowledges the use of the "Animated" characters and the right to use the "Animated" logo under copyright by Scopus Films, Israel.

ISBN: #0-943706-10-6

Printed in Israel

CONTENTS

* ASTERISK INDICATES RECIPE INTENDED FOR THE MORE EXPERIENCED COOK.

WHAT'S KOSHER ALL ABOUT?

This is one of the questions most often asked of religious Jews, probably because it is the most obvious example of what makes Jews different from the rest of the world.

The biblical reason for eating kosher is tied to the following verse: "You shall be holy because I am holy" (Leviticus 11:46). But what does "holy" mean? Ask any three people what they think of when they hear the word "holy" and each person will probably come up with a different answer.

One person might say: "Something holy is something that demands respect."

Another person might say: "Things holy have to do with G-d."

And yet the third person might say: "Someone holy is someone you don't mess with."

All three people have touched upon aspects of holiness which are true. But I think a good way to better understand the word holy, or "kadosh" as it is called in Hebrew, is to contrast it with the word "bracha", which means blessing.

A blessing is an abundance of the physical things we want: wealth, health, happiness, a good year. Holiness , however, is removing yourself from the physical , into the realm of the spiritual. Yom Kippur is called "Yom Hakodesh", The Holy Day, because you remove yourself from the material world completely, separating yourself from all food and material good.

For a religious Jew, life is always trying to find a path between blessing and holiness. We want the physical things that blessing brings and yet, if we are to become holy, we have to learn to separate ourselves from indulging our wants.

Being kosher is like that. We want to eat everything. We *need* this or that food to make us happy. G-d tells the Jew: "Fine. Eat food. I'll give you the blessing you want. But even in the physical act of eating you can be holy. How? By eating only what I tell you. By eating kosher."

I remember when my oldest daughter, Batya, was barely five years old and she was invited to a birthday party by a friend whose home was not kosher. She came to me with her problem. "Abba," she said, sadness in her voice, "I want to go to the party but half the fun is eating the food and treats. What should I do?"

"That's a difficult question, " I told her. "You can either stay home, or you can go and not eat, or you can go with a chocolate cupcake from home." Of course she took the third choice.

As she was walking away she suddenly turned, and with a smile, said: "Actually, I guess I'm pretty lucky Abba. My friend Bina is allergic to anything chocolate, and I'm only allergic to anything which is not kosher."

Kashrut. It teaches us we can't have everything we want. It shows us how to remove ourselves from the purely physical and come into contact with the Divine. It helps us to understand that even in a tuna fish salad there is a holy spark which enables us to elevate the simple act of digesting food into the spiritual act of nurturing our souls.

But there's even more to kashrut than this. Rabbi Samson Rafael Hirsch makes an important point when he says that the fowl which the Torah forbids us to eat are all birds of prey. They kill other birds and animals to survive. The fish which the Torah forbids us to eat, those without fins and scales, are the scavengers of the sea. The animals we eat are primarily domesticated. They do not kill each other in order to live. They live in harmony. According to Rabbi Hirsch, we have to learn from those animals we are permitted to eat how to behave in life. For most of us, the earlier we learn this lesson the better off we'll be.

And finally, as a religious Jew, the very fact that I choose what and how to eat in accordance with the Divine Will turns the supermarket where I shop, the kitchen where I prepare my food, and the dining room where I eat, into an extension of the study hall where I learn and the synagogue where I pray. I become, through my kashrut, a whole person, blessed by enjoying what I eat, and holy by knowing what to eat.

That's what kashrut is all about.

B'tayavon!

June 5, 1991
23 Sivan 5751

Rabbi Shlomo Riskin
Efrat, Israel

READ THIS FIRST

Cooking can be a lot of fun. Especially when you use *The Animated Children's Kosher Holiday Cookbook*. But before you get started there are a few important safety measures you should consider.

1. **Hot Oil**   Never drop food into hot oil. Foods that come into contact with hot oil usually create a brief "oil splatter". Little drops of oil fly out of the pan. Be careful. Using a metal spatula or spoon, gently let the food slide into the oil. Also, always face the handle of the pot or pan you are using away from the edge of the stove.

2. **Mitts**   Most "ouches" come from being in a hurry. It takes an extra minute to put on oven mitts but it's worth it. Pots and pans get hot quickly on or in the stove so when you remove them wear your mitts.

3. **Knives**   Knives are dangerous. Always cut on a cutting board, not on your hand. Make sure you don't leave a knife close to the edge of the table. Little brothers and sisters somehow always manage to find the most dangerous things to play with.

4. **Adults**   If this is your first time cooking, make sure an adult supervises you. A successful cook is one who knows what he or she is doing. Don't be embarrassed to take advice from an adult. Most parents want their kids to learn how to cook by themselves, so wait until they tell you you are ready to "solo".

5. **Hygiene**   Wash your hands before you start cooking. Pin up your hair if you have long hair. Remember, you wouldn't like dirt or hair in your food.

BASIC COOKING TERMS

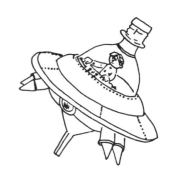

Here's a short glossary of some of the cooking terms we use in our cookbook. Try to remember them. They'll make cooking just a little bit easier.

Baste ✳ To moisten meats or poultry with a liquid. It's usually done during roasting.

Blend ✳ To mix two or more ingredients until smooth.

Boil ✳ To cook a liquid at boiling temperature (212 degrees). Bubbles rise continually breaking on the surface.

Bread ✳ To coat food in flour, egg and crumbs.

Broil ✳ To cook by direct heat, usually under heating unit (broiler) in oven.

Chop ✳ To cut into small pieces.

Fold ✳ To gently mix ingredients by turning one part over the other with a spatula.

Fry ✳ To cook in hot oil or butter.

Melt ✳ To heat until a solid becomes a liquid.

Whip ✳ To beat quickly with an egg beater, electric mixer, or wire whisk.

COOKING TIPS

Here are a few kitchen-tested cooking tips that both the beginner and "mayven" may find useful:

1) **Read the Whole Recipe**   The recipes in our cookbook are divided into three sections: *Ingredients, Utensils, How To Do It.* This makes it easier for you to see, at a glance, exactly what you need and how to cook a perfect dish each time. However, you should read and follow the recipe exactly as it is written. It's true, everyone likes to be creative, especially in the kitchen, but some recipes just won't work if you change them.

2) **Measure Carefully**   Take your time when you measure. Rushing usually means you end up with a mess and too little or too much of an ingredient. Here's how to measure:

Liquid Ingredients   Put the measuring cup on a level surface, then pour in as much liquid as the recipe calls for. Look through the cup with your eye at the same level as the liquid to make sure you have the right amount.

Dry Ingredients   Gently fill the measuring spoon or cup to overflowing with the ingredient. Don't pack it down or bang the spoon or cup. Then level the ingredient off with a spatula or table knife.

Butter or Margarine   Pack the ingredient into either the measuring spoon or dry measuring cup, then level it off with a spatula or table knife.

3) **How To Separate Egg Whites**   Gently crack the egg on the rim of a glass. Separate the shell halves slowly. Keep the yolk in one half of the shell. Pour the white from the other half of the shell into a small bowl. Slide the yolk into the empty half shell. Pour any leftover egg white into bowl. Put yolk into second bowl.

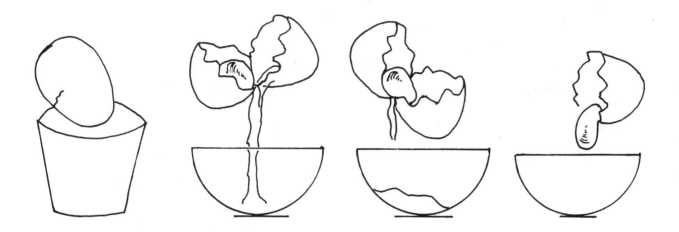

4) **How To Grease A Pan**   The best way to keep food from sticking to the pan is to spread a thin layer of oil on the bottom of the pan. This will save you long hours of scouring and scraping during cleanup.

Thanks....

An important Jewish concept is that of "Makir Tov", recognizing when someone does something good for you. In a cookbook as large as this one there are a lot of people who have helped to "put it all together".

Now is the time to acknowledge them.

The Cookbook Committee worked hard and diligently to coordinate and organize every aspect of this cookbook. *Nava Eizik, Lanie Klein, Ilana Myerson, Yocheved Rabin,* and *Tzila Rosenberg,* all from Efrat, deserve special thanks for their efforts.

Tasting and testing each recipe is no easy task. From hundreds of recipes submitted for our cookbook, the tasting/testing group only accepted the 80+ recipes found in this cookbook. Many a tongue was burned, and taste-buds screamed for surcease, but our intrepid group ate on, cooking and tasting recipe after recipe. Until, finally, **The Animated Children's Kosher Holiday Cookbook** was born.

Who were these indomitable taster/testers? I'm glad you asked. Here they are:

Yehudah Berman, Shulamit Berman, Merl Cohen, Seraya Demsky, Shelly Dwoletsky, Debra Elstein, Lisa Fredman, Micky Mirvis, Shlomo Peterseil, Tiferet Peterseil, and *Bruria Rabinowitz.*

We would also like to thank *Rami Peles* for his help with the graphics.

This cookbook is published by Ohr Torah Institutions in Israel. Ohr Torah is located in the Judean hills in the city of Efrat. Here, hundreds of students from high school through rabbinical school attend Ohr Torah Institutions. In just eight years Ohr Torah has blossomed into a major center for Jewish education.

Rabbi Shlomo Riskin, who has written the Introduction to this cookbook, is the founder and dean of Ohr Torah Institutions. His ability to speak to Jews of every persuasion about the centrality of Torah and the Land of Israel to the future of our people, has become legendary. He is a leading spokesman for Torah with Derech Eretz.

With such mentors, and such helpers, We're certain **The Animated Children's Kosher Holiday Cookbook** is destined for success.

Enjoy,

Yaacov Peterseil
Rivka Demsky

16

SHABBAT

Our Rabbis tell us that G-d said to the world, "I have a most precious jewel in my storehouse which I want to give to the Jewish People. This jewel is called Shabbat."

The Shabbat is the most precious day of the week to the Jew. On this day, a Jew leaves go of the world around him and floats joyously on a cloud of peace and harmony. For 24 hours the Jew gives his soul a chance to breathe. He learns Torah and frees his mind from the problems of the week.

On Shabbat we stop worrying about school and work. We start thinking about how to become better people and how to tune into the beauty that is G-d's world.

Date: Every 7th Day from B'raisheet

Basic Mitzvot:

Kiddush -- On Friday night we say a special prayer that ushers in the Shabbat. We say this prayer with a cup of wine.

Candles -- On Friday night we light candles. They symbolize the peace and harmony we want in our homes on Shabbat. Usually, women light the candles.

Rest -- There are many mitzvot that involve the special Shabbat style of resting. This type of rest usually means you have to keep away from many of the activities you do during the week.

Havdalah -- The ceremony that takes place on Shabbat night after three stars appear in the sky. Blessings are said on a multi-wick candle, spices, and wine.

3 Meals -- One meal is eaten on Friday night, another on Shabbat during the day, and the third meal, known as "seudah shlisheet", is eaten before sundown.

Customs and Symbols:

Challot -- Two special loaves of bread are eaten at each of the three Shabbat meals.

Red Wine -- Sweet red wine is drunk on Friday night and Shabbat morning after synagogue.

Blessing Children -- Many parents bless their childen on Friday night when everyone is around the Shabbat table.

Z'mirot -- Songs are sung at the Shabbat table.

Finger Lickin' Bar-B-Q Chicken

MEAT

Serves 4

Ingredients

1 chicken cut into 8 pieces
1 onion
3 tablespoons oil for frying
3/4 cup ketchup
3/4 cup water
3 tablespoons brown sugar
1/3 cup lemon juice
1/4 teaspoon salt

Utensils

measuring cups
measuring spoons
casserole dish
knife
cutting board
pot
bowl
spoon

Rabbi Menahem-Mendel of Kotzk, one of the great Hassidic Rabbis, was once asked why he never wrote a book. The Rabbi replied: "Let's say I write a book. Who is going to buy it? My disciples. And when will they find time to read it? They learn all week. So that leaves Shabbat. On Shabbat they go to synagogue, come home, eat a big Shabbat meal and only then do they have time to read. My disciples will pick up my book and on a full stomach will soon fall asleep. Now, tell me, what am I to write a book for? To help my disciples fall asleep?"

How To Do It

1. Put chicken into casserole dish.
2. Peel onion. Cut onion into small pieces with knife on cutting board.
3. Heat oil in pot.
4. Fry chopped onion till light brown.
5. Put ketchup, water, sugar, lemon juice and salt into bowl. Mix well with spoon.
6. Add ketchup mixture to pot. Cook on medium heat for 5 minutes.
7. Pour sauce evenly over chicken.
8. Bake at 350 degrees Fahrenheit for 1 hour.

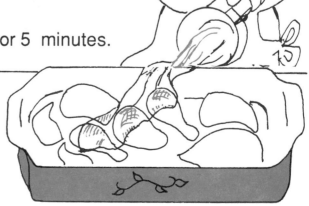

Shake To Bake Chicken

Serves 4

Ingredients

1/2 cup flour
1/2 teaspoon paprika
1/2 teaspoon salt
1 chicken cut into 8 pieces
1 teaspoon oil for greasing

Utensils

measuring cups
measuring spoons
plastic bag and tie
plate
roasting pan

How To Do It

1. Put the flour, paprika and salt into the plastic bag. Tie the bag and shake all the ingredients together till well blended.
2. Open bag. Put 2 pieces of chicken into plastic bag. Tie bag again and shake well to coat chicken on all sides with the flour mixture. Put the two pieces on a plate.
3. Repeat this process till all the chicken pieces are coated with the flour mixture.
4. Grease the roasting pan.
5. Place chicken pieces in roasting pan skin side up.
6. Bake at 425 degrees Fahrenheit for 1-1/2 hours or till golden brown.

Tantalizing Schnitzel

MEAT

Serves 6

Ingredients

6 medium chicken cutlets
1 cup italian dressing
2 cups corn flake crumbs
3/4 cup flour
2 eggs
1/2 cup oil for frying

Utensils

measuring cups
casserole dish
3 bowls
frying pan
fork
spatula
paper towel
plate

Q. Why do we use 2 challot on Shabbat?

A. Because we received a double portion of mannah for Shabbat in the desert.

How To Do It

1. Put cutlets into casserole dish.
2. Pour italian dressing into casserole dish over cutlets.   Refrigerate for 4 hours.
3. Remove casserole dish from refrigerator. Drain off excess dressing.
4. Put flour into first bowl and corn flake crumbs into second bowl.
5. Put eggs into third bowl. Beat well with fork.
6. Dip cutlet into flour then into eggs and finally into corn flake crumbs. Repeat till all cutlets are breaded.
7. Heat oil in frying pan.
8. Using a fork, gently put cutlets into frying pan. Fry cutlets about 5 minutes or till bottom is golden brown. Turn cutlets over with spatula and fry another 5 minutes or till other side is golden brown.
9. Put paper towel on plate. With spatula, remove cutlets from frying pan. Place on paper towel to drain till ready to serve.

Fancy Tuna Quiche

DAIRY

Serves 6

Ingredients

1 onion
1 green pepper
1 tablespoon margarine for frying
1 6-1/2 oz. can tuna
9" pie crust
4 eggs
1 cup sour cream

Utensils

measuring cups
measuring spoons
knife
cutting board
frying pan
can opener
fork
spoon
bowl

The Chelm Kids Take A Bath
Part One:
The children of Chelm hated baths. So, the wise men of Chelm met to decide what to do.
" Our children hate to bathe," Reb Yankel explained, "but they must be clean for Shabbat. What should we do?"
"I've got it!" yelled Reb Bindel, "we'll give them dry baths. They can go to the river but not have to dunk in. That way they won't complain about being wet or cold." Everyone clapped. Except Reb Zundel.
"Fool!" he called out. "If they don't get wet, how will they dry themselves!" Everyone couldn't help but agree.

How To Do It

1. Preheat oven to 350 degrees Fahrenheit for 15 minutes.
2. Peel onion. Wash pepper. Cut onion and pepper into small pieces with knife on cutting board.
3. Heat margarine in frying pan.
4. Fry onion and pepper till tender but not brown. Remove frying pan from heat.
5. Drain liquid from can of tuna. Add tuna to frying pan. Mix well with fork.
6 Spoon tuna mixture into pie crust.
7. Put 4 eggs into bowl. Beat with fork. Add sour cream to bowl. Mix well. Pour over tuna mixture.
8. Bake for 35 minutes.

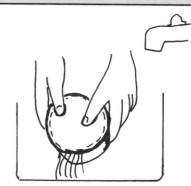

22

Use Your Noodle Koogle

Ingredients

1 lb. medium broad egg noodles
5 eggs
1 stick margarine
1/2 cup sugar
1 cup orange juice

Utensils

measuring cups
colander
mixing bowl
fork
large pot
medium casserole dish

Rabbi Pinchas, the Tzaddik of Koritz, used to say that the Jews eat lots of lokshen (noodles) on Shabbat because noodles are symbolic of the unity of the people of Israel: They are so entangled that they can never be separated.

How To Do It

1. Boil 2 quarts water in pot. Place noodles into boiling water. Stir with fork. Cook noodles on medium heat till soft.
2. Put colander into sink. Pour spaghetti into colander to drain.
3. Put noodles into bowl.
4. Add margarine to bowl. Mix well with fork.
5. Add eggs, sugar and orange juice to bowl. Mix well.
6. Pour noodle mixture into casserole dish.
7. Bake at 400 degrees Fahrenheit for 45 minutes.

23

L'il Devil Eggs

Serves 2

Ingredients

2 eggs
2 teaspoons mayonnaise
1/2 teaspoon ketchup
paprika for sprinkling

Utensils

measuring spoons
small pot
knife
cutting board
teaspoon
bowl
fork

Q. What is the last meal on Shabbat called?
A. Seudah Shlisheet

How To Do It

1. Put eggs into small pot. Add enough water to cover eggs. Boil eggs for 10 minutes.
2. Run cold water over eggs in pot. Peel hard boiled eggs.
3. Cut the eggs in half lengthwise with knife on cutting board. Using a teaspoon, carefully remove yolks from eggs without breaking the whites. Put yolks into bowl.
4. Mash the egg yolks with fork. Add mayonnaise and ketchup and mix well.
5. Put the egg yolk mixture back into the egg whites.
6. Sprinkle eggs with paprika.

24

Cherry Cake

Ingredients

2 eggs
1 cup sugar
1 teaspoon vanilla
1/2 cup oil
3 tablespoons water
1-1/2 cup flour
2 teaspoons baking powder
21 oz. can Mrs. Wyman's cherry filling
oil for greasing

Utensils

measuring cups
measuring spoons
electric mixer
mixer bowl
tablespoon
9 inch square baking pan
rubber spatula
can opener

How To Do It

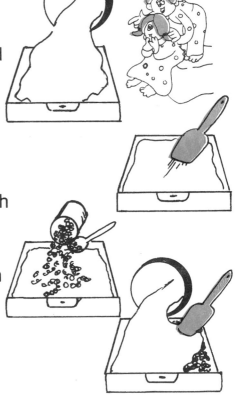

1. Put eggs, sugar and vanilla into mixer bowl. Beat on medium speed till mixture is smooth.
2. Add oil to mixer bowl. Beat on medium speed till mixture is smooth.
3. Add water, flour and baking powder to mixer bowl. Beat on low speed till cake mixture is well blended.
4. Grease baking pan.
5. Pour half of cake mixture into baking pan. Spread evenly in pan with rubber spatula
6. Spoon pie filling into baking pan.
7. Pour remaining cake mixture into baking pan. Spread evenly in pan with rubber spatula.
8. Bake at 350 degrees Fahrenheit for 50 minutes or till brown.

Mr. Potato Salad PARVE

Serves 8

Ingredients

1 small onion
4 potatoes
1 celery stalk
1 green or red pepper
2 eggs
1 teaspoon salt
1/2 teaspoon paprika
1/2 cup mayonnaise
1 teaspoon parsley

Utensils

measuring cups
measuring spoons
knife
potato peeler
cutting board
mixing bowl
pot with lid
fork
deep bowl
large plate

How To Do It

1. Peel onion and potatoes. Wash potatoes, celery and pepper.
2. Cut onion, celery, and pepper into small pieces with knife on cutting board. Put into bowl.
3. Boil eggs in pot for twelve minutes. Remove pot from heat. Run cold water from tap over eggs till cool.
4. Peel eggs. Add to bowl and mash with fork.
5. Put potatoes into pot. Add water to cover potatoes. Put lid on pot.
6. Boil potatoes for 20 minutes or till soft enough to pierce with fork.
7. Remove potatoes from pot with slotted spoon and put them on plate. Cool.
8. Cut potatoes into cubes with knife on cutting board. Add to bowl.
9. Gently mix potatoes, vegetables and mashed eggs with fork.

10. Add salt, paprika and mayonnaise.
11. Put salad into deep bowl. Pack salad down with fork.
12. Refrigerate for at least 1 hour.
13. Turn bowl of salad upside down onto a large plate. Carefully remove bowl.
14. Sprinkle pieces of parsley on top of salad in shape of smiley.

The Chelm Kids Take A Bath
Part Two:
"We must decide what to do," Reb Yontif announced. "Our children don't want to take baths every Shabbat." Everyone thought. For days they thought. Finally, Reb Yid, the math expert of Chelm explained. "Every fool knows that whether you save fifty coins during a year or you find fifty coins all at once, it's all the same. You have fifty coins." Everyone nodded. Even those who didn't understand. "It's no different with baths. Our children don't have to take their baths week after week. Let them take a whole year's worth of baths all at once." So, that Friday the kids of Chelm took fifty two baths. And for the rest of the year not one child complained... About a bath.

Yossef Mokir Shabbat Salad

Serves 4

PARVE

Ingredients

1 cucumber
1 stalk of celery
3 slices fresh or canned pineapple
1 sour pickle
8 pitted olives
1 6-1/2 oz. can tuna fish
1/2 cup mayonnaise

Utensils

measuring cups
potato peeler
knife
cutting board
bowl
can opener
fork

> Yosef was very poor. But whatever money he saved during the week he would use on Friday to buy the biggest fish he could find for Shabbat. "This makes my Shabbat special," Yosef would announce every Friday night to his family. Yosef worked for a greedy man named Sorav. Sorav made Yosef work hard and paid him very little. One night Sorav dreamed that he would lose all his money. So, early in the morning Sorav bought a giant diamond in exchange for all the money he owned. With this diamond Sorav set sail for lands far away. "Safe at last," he said to himself as he admired his diamond. 🖝 🖝

How To Do It

1. Peel cucumber. Wash cucumber and celery.
2. Cut cucumber, celery, pineapple and pickle into small pieces with knife on cutting board. Put into bowl.
3. Cut olives in half. Add to bowl.
4. Drain liquid from tuna. Add tuna and mayonnaise to bowl.
5. Mix all ingredients together with fork.

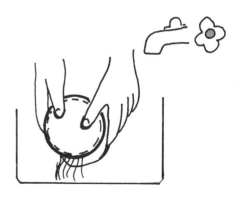

28

Beany Salad

Serves 8

Ingredients

1 medium onion
1 can yellow string beans
1 can green string beans
1 can baked beans in tomato sauce
1/3 cup vinegar
2/3 cup oil
1/2 teaspoon salt
1/4 teaspoon pepper
1/4 teaspoon garlic powder
1/4 teaspoon dry mustard powder
1 teaspoon sugar

Utensils

measuring cups
measuring spoons
knife
mixing bowl
can opener
bowl
cutting board
fork

But just then a storm rocked the boat and Sorav and the diamond fell overboard. A big fish saw the glare of the diamond and thought it was another fish. Quickly the big fish swallowed the diamond. And just as quickly it found itself trapped in a net the fishermen had spread in the sea. That Friday Yosef went to the market as usual to buy his fish. "Look at this great fish," one of the fishermen said, "isn't it beautiful!" Yosef saw the fish and said, " I must have it. I must! Here is all the money I own. Please give me the fish." The fisherman took the money and gave Yosef the fish. When Yosef arrived home he was so happy. "Look at this wonderful fish," he told his wife, "surely it is the best fish in the world." His wife smiled and took the fish. When she cut it open she found...the diamond. And from that day on Yosef had enough money to make the Shabbat meal special for himself, his family, and all his friends.

How To Do It

1. Peel onion. Cut into small pieces with knife on cutting board. Put onion into mixing bowl.
2. Drain liquid from cans of string beans. Put string beans into bowl.
3. Add baked beans to bowl.
4. Put vinegar, oil, salt, pepper, garlic powder,mustard powder and sugar into second bowl.
5. Mix well with fork.
6. Pour vinegar mixture into mixing bowl.
7. Mix well.

ROSH HASHANAH

Rosh Hashanah, the Jewish "New Year", is the time we begin to think about our relationships with other people and with G-d. This 10 day period of self-examination and repentance reaches a peak on Yom Kippur, the Day of Atonement.

Date: 1st of Tishrei

Basic Mitzvot:

Shofar -- We listen to the blowing of the shofar.

Repentance -- We ask forgiveness from anyone we may have harmed by our words or actions.

Customs and Symbols:

New Year Greetings -- At the end of the evening service in synagogue we say to one another, "May you be inscribed and sealed for a good year".

Honey -- We dip a piece of challah or a slice of apple in honey and say, " May it be G-d's will to renew for us a year that will be good and sweet".

Bubby's Baked Apples

PARVE

Serves 4

> On Rosh Hashanah the world was created, and on Rosh Hashanah our Forefathers were born.

Ingredients

4 medium apples
1/4 cup sugar
4 teaspoons raisins
2 tablespoons margarine
1/2 cup water

Utensils

measuring cups
measuring spoons
apple corer
baking pan with lid
spoon

How To Do It

1. Core the apples most of the way through. Put apples in baking pan.
2. Divide sugar into 4 parts and put one part into the hole of each apple.
3. Put 1 teaspoon of raisins and 1/2 teaspoon of margarine into each apple.
4. Put water into baking pan.
5. Cover pan and bake at 350 degrees Fahrenheit for 45 minutes.

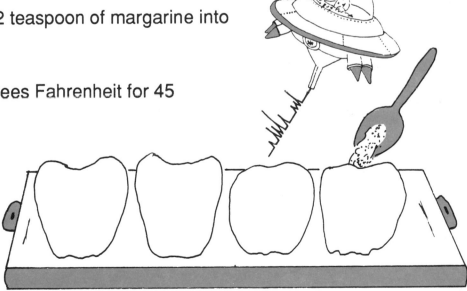

A Honey of a Chicken

MEAT

Serves 4

Ingredients

1 chicken cut into 8 pieces
1/2 small onion
1 clove garlic
1 tablespoon lemon juice
2 tablespoons soy sauce
3/4 cup honey
1/2 teaspoon salt
1/4 teaspoon dry mustard
1/4 teaspoon pepper

Utensils

measuring cups
measuring spoons
roasting pan
cutting board
small pot
tablespoon

Q. What are other names for Rosh Hashanah?

A. Yom Ha'Zikaron -- Day of Remembrance
Yom Teruah -- Day of Sounding the Shofar

Q. What are the 10 days between Rosh Hashanah and Yom Kippur called?

A. Aseret Y'may Teshuvah -- Ten Days of Repentance

How To Do It

1. Place chicken pieces in roasting pan.
2. Peel onion and garlic. Cut onion and garlic into small pieces with knife on cutting board. Put into pot.
3. Add all remaining ingredients to pot. Cook till sauce begins to boil. Remove from heat.
4. Pour the sauce evenly over chicken.
5. Bake at 350 degrees Fahrenheit.
6. Baste the chicken every half hour with a tablespoon.
7. Bake for 1-1/2 hours or till chicken is nicely browned.

Saucy Chicken

MEAT

Serves 4

Ingredients

1/2 cup barbecue sauce
1/4 cup grape jam
1 chicken for frying cut into 8

Utensils

measuring cups
bowl
spoon
roasting pan
fork

Q. What do we call the three sounds of the shofar?

A. Tekiah - a long drawn-out sound
Shevarim - a broken, sad sound
Teruah - a series of sharp, staccato sounds

Q. How many blasts are sounded on the shofar?

A. 100

How To Do It

1. Put barbecue sauce and jam into bowl. Mix with spoon.
2. Dip chicken into jam mixture to coat well on all sides.
3. Place chicken in roasting pan, skin side up.
4. Pour any remaining sauce over chicken.
5. Bake at 350 degrees Fahrenheit for 1-1/2 hours or till chicken is easily pierced with fork.

33

Sweet Potato Fluff

Serves 8

Ingredients

5 sweet potatoes
2 eggs
2 tablespoons matza meal
1 teaspoon salt
1/4 cup orange juice
1 teaspoon cinnamon
1/4 cup sugar
10 kosher marshmallows
oil for greasing

Utensils

measuring cups
measuring spoons
potato peeler
knife
cutting board
pot with lid
fork
slotted spoon
bowl
wooden spoon
baking pan

How To Do It

1. Peel and wash sweet potatoes.
2. Cut potatoes into small pieces with knife on cutting board.
3. Put potatoes into pot. Add water to cover potatoes. Put lid on pot.
4. Boil for 20 minutes or till soft enough to pierce with fork.
5. Take potatoes out of pot with slotted spoon and put into bowl. Drain water from bowl.
6. Mash potatoes with fork.
7. Add eggs, matza meal, salt, juice, cinnamon and sugar, one at a time and mix thoroughly with wooden spoon after each addition.
8. Grease baking pan.
9. Pour sweet potato mixture into baking pan.

34

10. Bake at 350 degrees Fahrenheit for 1/2 hour. Carefully remove baking pan from oven.
11. Cover sweet potato mixture with marshmallows.
12. Bake another 10 minutes or till marshmallows are browned.

Originally the shofar was blown on the morning of Rosh Hashanah. Many years ago some rulers thought the shofar was a call to battle and that the Jews would attack. In the morning soldiers were placed in front of each synagogue to make sure the shofar would not be blown. Later in the day, when the soldiers left, we were able to blow the shofar, and this custom has remained.

Candied Sweet Potatoes

PARVE

Serves 4-6

Ingredients

2 large sweet potatoes
1 teaspoon salt
1/4 cup margarine
1/2 cup brown sugar
1 cup water
1/4 cup orange juice

Utensils

measuring cups
measuring spoons
potato peeler
knife
cutting board
pot with lid
small pot
roasting pan

How To Do It

1. Peel sweet potatoes with potato peeler.
2. Cut each potato lengthwise into 4 slices with knife on cutting board. Now cut each of the slices in half.
3. Put sweet potatoes into pot with lid. Add water to cover potatoes.
4. Add salt. Cover pot.
5. Cook potatoes till water boils. Turn off heat. Let potatoes stand in boiling water.
6. Put margarine, brown sugar, water and orange juice into second pot. Cook till sauce boils.
7. Take sweet potatoes out of water and put them into roasting pan.
8. Pour sauce evenly over sweet potatoes.
9. Bake at 300 degrees Fahrenheit for 1/2 hour or till potatoes are soft.

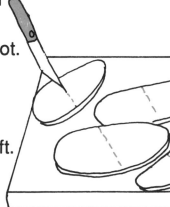

Top Banana Cake

PARVE

Ingredients

1 teaspoon oil for greasing
1 cup sugar
1/2 cup margarine
2 eggs
1/2 cup orange juice
3 bananas
1 teaspoon vanilla
1-1/2 teaspoons baking soda
1-1/2 cups flour
1 cup chocolate chips

Utensils

measuring cups
measuring spoons
electric mixer
mixer bowl
fork
small bowl
9 inch tube pan

How To Do It

1. Grease baking pan.
2. Mix sugar and margarine together in the mixer bowl on medium speed till well blended.
3. Peel and then mash the bananas with a fork in small bowl.
4. Add remaining ingredients one by one to mixer bowl in the order they are listed. Be sure to mix well on medium speed after each addition.
5. Pour mixture into baking pan.
6. Bake at 350 degrees Fahrenheit for 40 minutes or till golden brown.

Lemon Icing PARVE

Ingredients

2 cups confectioners sugar
2 teaspoons vanilla
3 tablespoons lemon juice

Utensils

measuring cups
measuring spoons
bowl
fork
rubber spatula

On Rosh Hashanah G-d judges the world. Three books are opened. Those who are evil are immediately inscribed for Death. Those who are righteous are immediately inscribed for Life. Those in-between, the majority of us, are given a chance during the 10 Days of Repentance to do teshuvah.

How To Do It

1. Put sugar, vanilla and lemon juice into bowl.
2. Mix together with fork. If mixture is too thick, add one or two tablespoons of water.
3. Spread evenly on cake with spatula.

Batter - Up!

Serves 2

Ingredients

2 large apples
1/4 cup sugar
4 tablespoons lemon juice
1 egg
1 cup flour
1/2 teaspoon salt
2 teaspoons baking powder
1/2 cup milk
oil for frying

Utensils

measuring cups
measuring spoons
knife
cutting board
bowl
mixing bowl
fork
frying pan
spatula
plate
paper towel

How To Do It

1. Wash, core and peel apples. Cut apples into round slices with knife on cutting board. Put into bowl.
2. Sprinkle sugar and lemon juice on apples. Let stand 1/2 hour.
3. Put egg and milk into small bowl. Beat together with fork.
4. Put flour, salt and baking powder into mixing bowl. Add egg mixture. Mix with fork till mixture is smooth.
5. Heat oil in frying pan.
6. Dip apple slices into flour batter. Using the spatula, gently put apple slices into hot oil. Fry till brown on bottom. Turn apples over with spatula and fry till other side is brown.
7. Put paper towel on plate. Remove apples from frying pan with spatula. Place fried apples on paper towel to drain till ready to serve.

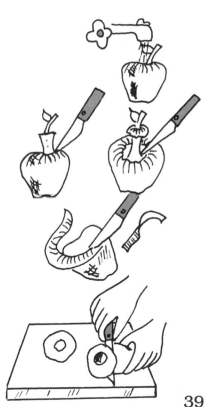

Strawberry Fluff

PARVE

Serves 6-8

Ingredients

2 boxes strawberries
2 egg whites
4 tablespoons sugar
1/4 teaspoon cream of tartar

Utensils

measuring spoons
colander
electric mixer
mixer bowl
small bowl
freezer container

How To Do It

1. Remove stems from strawberries.
2. Put colander into sink.
3. Put strawberries into colander and wash gently with cold water.
4. Put strawberries into mixer bowl.
5. Beat on medium speed till strawberries are crushed. Put into small bowl.
6. Wash and dry mixer bowl.
7. Put egg whites into mixer bowl.
8. Add cream of tartar to mixer bowl.
9. Beat till egg whites are stiff, constantly adding sugar a little at a time to mixer bowl.
10. Add crushed strawberries to mixer bowl. Beat 10 minutes.
11. Pour strawberry mixture into freezer container. Freeze overnight.
12. Remove strawberry fluff from freezer 45 minutes before serving time.

Bubbly Champagne

Serves 8

Ingredients

3/4 cup sugar
1 cup water
1 cup grapefruit juice
1/2 cup orange juice
1 quart cold ginger ale

Utensils

measuring cups
pot
spoon
bowl

Q. What is the name of the Shabbat that falls out between Rosh Hashanah and Yom Kippur?

A. Shabbat Teshuvah -- Shabbat of Repentance, or Shabbat of Return

How To Do It

1. Put sugar and water into pot. Boil for 5 minutes. Cool.
2. Pour sugar and water into bowl.
3. Add grapefruit and orange juices to bowl.
4. Put into refrigerator for at least 2 hours.
5. At serving time, mix with spoon and then gently pour ginger ale into bowl.
6. Serve in champagne glasses.

Sukkot

Sukkot means "booths" or "temporary huts". The Children of Israel lived in Sukkot during their 40 years in the desert. But the real importance of Sukkot is in the fact that we leave our homes and move into temporary dwellings as a sign of our trust in G-d's protection.

Date: 15th of Tishrei

Basic Mitzvot:

Living in a Sukkah -- Includes eating and sleeping in the sukkah.

Lulav and Etrog -- Includes 2 willow branches (aravot) and 3 myrtle branches (hadasim) tied to the lulav.

Customs and Symbols:

Sukkah Decorations -- We decorate the sukkah to make it cheerful and inviting.

Ushpizin -- We invite one of 7 "guests" into the sukkah each evening. Avraham, Yitzchak, Yaacov, Moshe, Aharon, Yosef, and David.

Corn Soup

Serves 6

Ingredients

2 large onions
2 potatoes
1 teaspoon dill
4 tablespoons butter for frying
2 tablespoons flour
2 cups water
2 teaspoons salt
4 cups milk
1 cup corn niblets

Utensils

measuring cups
measuring spoons
potato peeler
knife
cutting board
large pot
wooden spoon

Q. What is the name of the holiday which celebrates the finishing of the reading of the Torah?

A. Simchat Torah

Q. Why does a Sukkah not require a mezuzah?

A. Because it is a temporary, not a permanent, dwelling

How To Do It

1. Peel onions. Peel and wash potatoes.
2. Cut potatoes and onions into small pieces with knife on cutting board.
3. Wash dill and cut into small pieces on cutting board.
4. Heat butter in pot.
5. Fry onions in pot for 10 minutes or till soft but not brown. Mix well with wooden spoon.
6. Add flour to pot. Mix well.
7. Add water and salt to pot and mix.
8. Add potatoes, milk, corn and dill to pot.
9. Continue to cook soup on medium heat for an additional 1/2 hour, stirring occasionally with wooden spoon.

Spaghetti S'chach

DAIRY

Serves 6

Ingredients

2 quarts water
1 lb. spaghetti
1 large onion
1 teaspoon paprika
1 teaspoon sugar
1/2 teaspoon garlic powder
1 teaspoon salt
1/2 teaspoon pepper
1/4 teaspoon dry mustard powder
2 large cans crushed tomatoes
2 cups shredded cheddar cheese

Utensils

measuring cups
measuring spoons
large pot
colander
casserole dish
knife
cutting board
wooden spoon
can opener
fork

How To Do It

1. Boil 2 quarts water in pot. Place spaghetti into boiling water. Stir with fork. Cook spaghetti on medium heat till soft.
2. Put colander into sink. Pour spaghetti into colander to drain. Rinse spaghetti with cold water.
3. Put spaghetti into casserole dish.
4. Peel onions and cut into small pieces with knife on cutting board.
5. Heat oil in pot.
6. Fry onions for 15 minutes or till soft but not brown. Mix well with wooden spoon.
7. Add paprika, sugar, garlic, salt and pepper to pot. Mix well.
8. Add crushed tomatoes to pot. Mix well. Cook sauce on low heat for an additional 5 minutes.
9. Remove pot from heat.
10. Pour sauce into casserole dish. Mix well with fork.
11. Sprinkle cheddar cheese on top of casserole dish.
12. Bake at 350 degrees Fahrenheit for 1/2 hour.

44

Rainy Day Omelette

Serves 2

Ingredients

2 eggs
1/4 teaspoon salt
1/4 teaspoon pepper
1 tomato
3 mushrooms
1 onion
2 ozs. butter for frying

Utensils

measuring spoons
mixing bowl
slotted spoon
fork
knife
spatula
frying pan
cutting board

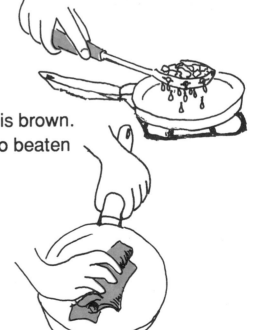

Q. What special prayer is said on Shmini Atzeret?

A. The Prayer for Rain.

Q. What parts of the Torah are read on Simchat Torah?

A. The last chapters of Deuteronomy and the beginning of Genesis.

Q. What is the "preferred" time for building the Sukkah?

A. Immediately after Yom Kippur.

How To Do It

1. Put eggs into mixing bowl. Add salt and pepper. Beat with fork till well mixed.
2. Wash tomato and mushrooms. Peel onion.
3. Cut tomato, mushrooms and onion, into small pieces with knife on cutting board.
4. Put half the butter into frying pan and heat. Fry onion, tomato and mushrooms in butter on medium heat till onion is brown.
5. Take vegetables out of frying pan with slotted spoon. Add to beaten egg. Mix well with fork.
6. Let frying pan cool. Clean frying pan with paper towel.
7. Heat remaining butter in frying pan.
8. Pour egg mixture back into frying pan. Fry till eggs are brown on bottom. With spatula, turn omelette over and fry till other side is brown.

45

Something Fishy

PARVE

Serves 4

Ingredients

2 lb. fresh fish fillets (halibut, sole, flounder)
1 fresh lemon
1 teaspoon salt
2 red peppers
2 celery stalks
2 onions
1/4 cup oil
1 teaspoon coriander
1 teaspoon turmeric
1/2 teaspoon cumin
1/4 cup water

Utensils

measuring cups
measuring spoons
plate
knife
cutting board
frying pan with lid
wooden spoon

Q. What does the rule "more shade than sunlight" refer to?

A. The thickness of the s'chach on the Sukkah.

Q. What day during Sukkot is it forbidden to take a lulav?

A. Shabbat

How To Do It

1. Place fish fillets on plate.
2. Squeeze lemon and sprinkle salt onto fish.
3. Wash red peppers, and celery.
4. Cut onions, peppers and celery into small pieces with knife on cutting board.
5. Heat oil in frying pan.
6. Fry onions, peppers and celery on low heat for 20 minutes or till soft. Mix well with wooden spoon.
7. Add coriander, tumeric and cumin to frying pan. Mix well.
8. Remove frying pan from heat.
9. Drain lemon juice from fish. Put fish into frying pan on top of vegetables.
10. Add water to frying pan. Cover frying pan.
11. Cook on low heat for about 15 minutes or till soft.

Meatball Magic

MEAT

Serves 4

Ingredients

1 lb. ground beef
1/2 cup flavored bread crumbs
1 large egg
1 can peas with liquid
1/2 cup water
1 large can tomato sauce
4 carrots
4 potatoes
1 small onion
oil for frying

Utensils

measuring cups
measuring spoons
bowl
large pot with lid
tablespoon
can opener
potato peeler
knife
cutting board

Q. Why is the last day of Sukkot called "Simchat Torah"?

A. Because on this day we conclude the reading of the Torah.

Q. On Hoshana Rabba, how many times do we circle the Torah?

A. 7

How To Do It

1. Mix meat, bread crumbs and egg in large bowl.
2. Heat oil in pot .
3. Shape meat mixture into small balls (see illustration).
4. With spoon, gently place meat balls into heated oil. Fry meatballs till brown. Turn off heat.
5. Put peas, water and tomato sauce into pot.
6. Peel and wash carrots, potatoes and onion. Slice carrots with knife on cutting board. Cut potatoes and onion into small pieces on cutting board. Add carrots, potatoes and onion to pot.
7. Cover pot and simmer on low heat for about 1 hour. Add more water if necessary.

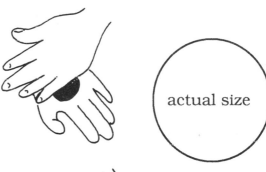

actual size

Mount of Olives Chicken

Serves 4

Ingredients

1 chicken cut into 8 pieces
1 onion
2 cloves garlic
3 tablespoons oil for frying
1/2 cup pitted olives
2 tablespoons tomato puree
1/2 cup water
1/2 tablespoon vinegar
1/4 cup raisins

Utensils

measuring cups
measuring spoons
casserole dish with lid
knife
cutting board
small pot
wooden spoon

Q. What do we call the last day of Sukkot?

A. Hoshanah Rabbah

Q. What occurs during the prayers of "Hoshanot"?

A. Everyone with a lulav and etrog joins in a procession around the bimah.

Q. In how many directions do we shake the lulav?

A. 6

How To Do It

1. Put chicken pieces into casserole dish.
2. Peel onions and garlic. Cut into small pieces with knife on cutting board.
3. Heat oil in pot.
4. Add onion and garlic to pot. Fry till onion is golden brown, stirring often with wooden spoon.
5. Add olives, puree, water, vinegar and raisins to pot.
6. Cook on low heat for 15 minutes, stirring often with wooden spoon.
7. Pour olive mixture evenly over chicken in casserole dish. Cover casserole dish.
8. Bake at 350 degrees Fahrenheit for 1-1/2 hours.

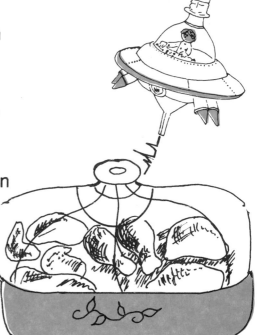

Lolly Ices

PARVE

Serves 6

Ingredients

3 bananas
3 oranges
3 lemons
3 cups sugar
3 cups water

Utensils

fork
juicer
bowl
ice tray
spoons

How To Do It

1. Mash bananas well with fork.
2. Squeeze oranges and lemons.
3. Put bananas, orange juice and lemon juice into bowl.
4. Add sugar and water to bowl. Mix well with spoon.
5. Put juice mixture into freezer.
6. Take mixture out of freezer every 1/2 hour and mix. Do this 4 times over a period of 2 hours.
7. Pour mixture into freezer ice tray.
8. Stick plastic spoons or regular teaspoons into each cube of the ice tray.
9. Freeze till juice mixture is frozen.

The Rabbi of Sadigura was sitting in his Sukkah eating, when he suddenly remembered he had forgotten to say the blessing "on sitting in the Sukkah." He was upset until one of his students came into the Sukkah and informed him that he had also forgotten to remove the glasss roof he used to protect the Sukkah from the rain. "Rabbi," the student gently admonished, "it seems that you haven't been eating in a kosher Sukkah." The Rabbi smiled. "Well, look on the bright side; at least I didn't say an unnecessary blessing on the Sukkah."

Polly Wanna Cracker Cake?

PARVE

Ingredients

10 oz. graham crackers
6-1/2 oz. margarine
2/3 cup sugar
1/2 cup cocoa
1 teaspoon vanilla
1 teaspoon rum extract
pinch of salt
2 eggs

Utensils

measuring cups
measuring spoons
bowl
pot
wooden spoon
plastic bag with tie

A TRUE STORY

Once a man built a Sukkah on the roof of the apartment he lived in. On the fourth day of Sukkot, the landlord approached him and was very upset. "I rent you an apartment," he yelled, "not a roof. If you don't take your little hut off this roof I'll take you to court." And that's exactly what he did. The judge heard what the landlord had to say and then asked the man why he had put a hut on the roof. "Thousands of years ago," the man said, "my people, the Jews, left Egypt where they were slaves and went into the desert where they lived in huts called sukkot.

How To Do It

1. Break crackers into very small pieces. Put into bowl.
2. Melt margarine in pot on low heat.
3. Add sugar to pot. Cook gently on low heat till sugar melts.
4. Remove pot from heat.
5. Add cocoa, vanilla, rum and salt to pot.
6. Add eggs to pot. Mix well with wooden spoon.
7. Pour mixture into bowl. Mix.
8. Spoon cookie mixture into plastic bag. Tie bag.
9. Shape cookie mixture into salami shape. Freeze.
10. Defrost 1/2 hour before serving. Serve sliced.

Heavenly Ice Cream

Serves 10

Ingredients

4 eggs
1 cup sugar
1 container parve cream for whipping
2 tablespoons sweetened cocoa

Utensils

measuring cups
measuring spoons
electric mixer
mixer bowl
large freezer container

How To Do It

1. Beat eggs and sugar in mixer bowl on highest speed for about 7 minutes or until the mixture is thick and white.
2. Add parve cream and continue beating till mixture is well blended.
3. Add sweetened cocoa and mix on low speed till blended.
4. Pour into freezer container and freeze.

Today, when Sukkot comes we remember how G-d took care of us in those huts by living in Sukkot as well. Your honor," the man concluded, "Sukkot only lasts another four days. Then I'll gladly take the Sukkah down." The judge thought and said. "Landlord, you are right. The Sukkah must come down. And come down it shall." Then he turned to the man. "Sir, you must take down your hut...within seven days. That is my ruling." The man thought for a moment. Then smiled.

Now Try These Flavors: *Substitute any of the following for #3*

1 teaspoon of vanilla extract and 1 tablespoon of cherry liquer.

1 teaspoon mint extract and 1/2 cup grated chocolate.

1 teaspoon rum extract and 1/2 cup raisins.

HANUKKAH

Hanukkah recalls the astonishing victory of the small army of the Maccabees against the forces of the Syrian-Greek Empire. For 3 years Mattityahu, the High Priest, and his 5 sons, led the Jews in a desperate battle for their spiritual and physical survival. Finally, the Jews conquered Israel and restored the holiness of the Temple by removing the idols of the Greeks.

Date: 25th of Kislev

Basic Mitzvot:

Lighting the Menorah -- When the Maccabees entered the Temple they could not find any pure oil to light the Temple Menorah. They searched until they found one small cruse of oil which had only enough oil for one day. A miracle happened and the oil lasted for 8 days. Today, we light the menorah at home adding a candle each night. We add candles from right to left, but we light the candles from left to right.

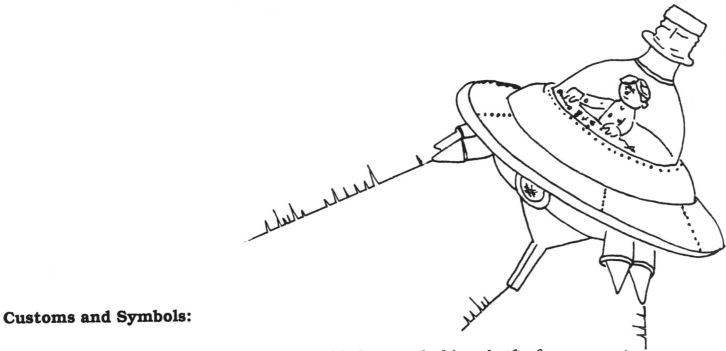

Customs and Symbols:

Hanukkah Gelt -- Children receive Hanukkah coins (gelt) and gifts from parents.

Playing Dreidle -- Children spin the dreidle (top) to see which letter it will land on. They put in their Hanukkah gelt. If the dreidle lands on Nun they get nothing. If on Gimel they get everything. If on Hey, they get half. If on Shin, they lose a turn. The letters stand for "A great miracle happened there". In Israel a Pey is substituted for a Shin to change the meaning to "A great miracle happened here."

Miracle Puff Pancakes

DAIRY

Serves 10-12

Ingredients

1 cup flour
1 teaspoon salt
2 teaspoons baking powder
1 egg
1 glass milk
oil for frying

Utensils

measuring cups
measuring spoons
bowl
fork
frying pan
tablespoon
spatula

A Jewish family once invited a poor man to their Hanukkah meal. The traditional "latkes" were served and the guest quickly took one and said: "This is in honor of the Lord of the Universe." Then he took two and said: "These are in honor of Moses and Aaron." Next he took three in honor of Abraham, Isaac and Jacob, and then four in honor of Sara, Rebecca, Rachel and Leah. The host turned to his wife and said: "You'd better take the latkes away; he may want to honor the 600,000 that Moses led out of Egypt."

How To Do It

1. Put flour, salt, and baking powder into bowl. Add egg. Mix well with fork.
2. Add milk slowly, constantly mixing with fork.
3. Let stand for 1/2 hour at room temperature.
4. Heat oil in frying pan.
5. Take a heaping tablespoonful of the flour pancake mixture and carefully place it in the hot oil. Repeat till all the potato mixture is used. Fry till pancakes are brown on bottom. With spatula, turn pancakes over and fry till other side is brown.

Potato Latkes

Serves 4

Ingredients

2 large potatoes
1 egg
1/2 teaspoon salt
2 tablespoons flour
2 tablespoons oil for frying

Utensils

measuring spoons
potato peeler
coarse grater or food processor
mixing bowl
tablespoon
frying pan
spatula
paper towel
flat plate

Q. In which town does the story of Hanukkah take place?

A. Modi'in

How To Do It

1. Peel and wash potatoes.
2. Grate the potatoes on a coarse grater or in a food processor, if you have one. Put the grated potatoes into mixing bowl.
3. Add egg, salt and flour to mixing bowl. Mix well.
4. Heat oil in frying pan.
5. Take a heaping tablespoonful of the latke mixture and carefully place it in the hot oil. Pat down latke with back of tablespoon. Repeat till all the potato mixture is used.
6. Fry till bottom is golden brown. Turn the latkes over with spatula and fry till other side is golden brown.
7. Put paper towel on plate. With spatula, remove latkes from frying pan. Place on paper towel to drain till ready to serve.

Victory Vege Pancakes

Serves 4

Ingredients

1 medium onion
1 stalk celery
1/2 cup mushrooms
1 tablespoon fresh dill
2 medium carrots
2 eggs
1/2 cup canned peas
2 tablespoons matza meal
1/2 teaspoon salt
1/4 teaspoon pepper
oil for frying

Utensils

measuring cups
measuring spoons
knife
cutting board
potato peeler
coarse grater
fork
small bowl
frying pan
mixing bowl
tablespoon
spatula
paper towel
plate

Our rabbis ask: "If there was already enough oil in the little cruse for 1 day, why don't we just celebrate Hanukkah for 7 days? " Some say that the minute the first candle was filled with oil the Jews noticed the cruse was filled again. Others say that the first candle really represents ☞ ☞ ☞

How To Do It

1. Peel onion. Wash celery, mushrooms and dill.
2. Cut onions, celery, mushrooms and dill into small pieces with knife on cutting board.
3. Wash and peel carrots. Grate carrots on coarse grater. Use 1 cup of grated carrots.
4. Put eggs into small bowl. Beat with fork.
5. Heat oil in frying pan.

6. Fry onion, celery and mushrooms for 10 minutes or till soft but not brown. Put into mixing bowl.
7. Add eggs, peas, matza meal, salt and pepper to bowl. Mix well with fork.
8. Take a heaping tablespoonful of the pancake mixture and carefully place it in frying pan. Repeat till all the potato mixture is used.
9. Fry till bottom is golden brown. With spatula turn pancakes over and fry till other side is golden brown.
10. Put paper towel on plate. With spatula, remove pancakes from frying pan. Place on paper towel to drain till ready to serve.

the miracle of defeating the Greeks. Still others answer that the Maccabees divided the oil into 8 parts so they would have a little oil for each night, but the oil burned all night on each of the 8 nights.

Coca Cola Chicken

MEAT

Serves 4

Ingredients

1 chicken cut into 8 pieces
1/4 cup apricot jam
1/4 cup ketchup
1/2 cup coca cola
1 teaspoon garlic powder
2 teaspoons soy sauce
3 tablespoons onion soup powder

Utensils

measuring cups
measuring spoons
casserole dish with lid
mixing bowl
spoon

Q. What 2 Hebrew words make up the word Hanukkah?

A. Hanu = they rested; kah = 25th. They Jews won the war on the 25th of Kislev.

Q. How many candles, in total, do we light on Hanukkah, including the Shamash?

A. 44

How To Do It

1. Put chicken in casserole dish.
2. Put jam and ketchup into bowl. Mix well with spoon.
3. Add coca cola, garlic powder, soy sauce and onion soup to bowl. Mix with spoon.
4. Pour coca cola mixture evenly over chicken. Cover casserole dish.
5. Bake at 350 degrees Fahrenheit for 1-1/2 hours.
6. Remove cover from casserole dish and bake chicken uncovered for another 1/2 hour.

Tain Lee Tuna

Serves 6

Ingredients

1 large can bean sprouts
1/4 small onion
6 eggs
1 teaspoon salt
1/2 teaspoon pepper
1 cup tuna
1 tablespoon cornstarch
3 tablespoons soy sauce
1 tablespoon sugar
1- 1/2 cups water
oil for frying

Utensils

measuring cups
measuring spoons
can opener
mixing bowl
knife
small bowl
fork
frying pan
spatula
plate
small pot

Q. What is the Shamash?

A. The extra candle we use each night to light the candles of the menorah.

Q. Why do we light the Hanukkah candles by the window?

A. So that people in the street will see and remember the miracle of the lights.

How To Do It

1. Drain liquid from can of bean sprouts. Put sprouts into bowl.
2. Peel the onion. Cut 1/4 of onion into small pieces with knife on the cutting board. Put into bowl.
3. Beat the eggs in a small bowl.
4. Add the eggs, salt, pepper, and tuna to bowl. Mix well with fork.
5. Heat oil in frying pan.
6. Pour ingredients from bowl into frying pan. Fry till tuna mixture turns brown on bottom. Turn over with spatula and fry till other side is golden brown.
7. Remove pan from heat. Using spatula, put fried tuna mixture on plate.
8. Put cornstarch, soy sauce, sugar and water into pot and heat. Stir constantly with spoon till sauce is thick. Remove from heat.
9. Pour sauce on tuna mixture.

Eye Toast You!

Serves 1

Ingredients

1 slice of white bread
1 egg
1/4 teaspoon salt
2 teaspoons of margarine for frying

Utensils

measuring spoons
frying pan
spatula
knife
plate

Q. Who were the Hellenists?

A. Jews who copied the lifestyle of the Greeks and brought Greek idols into the Temple.

Q. Which holiday is King Antiochus associated with?

A. Hanukkah.

How To Do It

1. Heat margarine in frying pan.
2. Fry bread in frying pan till bread turns brown on bottom. Turn bread over with spatula and fry till other side is golden brown.
3. Cut a small hole in the middle of the bread with sharp knife (see illustration). Put the slice of bread back into the frying pan.
5. Pour egg into the hole.
6. Sprinkle salt on egg.
7. Fry on low heat till egg is done.

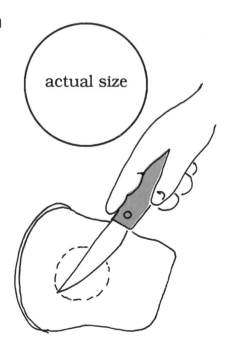

actual size

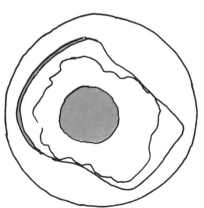

Salami Omelette

MEAT

Serves 2

Ingredients

1/4 small salami
1/4 small onion
2 eggs
1/4 teaspoon salt
2 tablespoons oil for frying

Utensils

measuring spoons
knife
cutting board
mixing bowl
small bowl
fork
frying pan
spatula

How To Do It

1. Cut salami into small pieces with knife on cutting board. Place into mixing bowl.
2. Peel onion. Cut into small pieces on cutting board. Add to bowl.
3. Beat the eggs in a small bowl with fork   Add salt. Add eggs to mixing bowl. Mix till all the ingredients are well blended.
4. Heat oil in frying pan.
5. Gently pour egg mixture into frying pan. Fry till bottom is brown. With spatula, turn omelette over and fry till other side is brown.

Jello Whip DAIRY

Serves 6-8

Ingredients

2 packages kosher jello
3 cups water
1 container whip cream

Utensils

measuring cups
bowl
small pot with lid
spoon

Q. Why do we eat latkes on Hanukkah?

A. Because they are fried in oil and oil reminds us of the miracle of Hanukkah.

Q. What basic mitzvah did the Greeks want the Jews to give up?

A. Brit (circumcision).

How To Do It

1. Put jello into bowl.
2. Pour water into small pot. Cover pot. Boil the water. Pour boiled water into the bowl. Mix with spoon till all the jello has dissolved. Cool.
3. Add whip cream to jello. Mix well.
4. Refrigerate for 2 hours before serving.

Bageleh

Serves 12

Ingredients

2 cups whole wheat flour
1 package dry yeast
1 teaspoon salt
1-1/3 cups hot tap water
1 tablespoon honey
2 cups white flour
oil for greasing

Utensils

measuring cups
measuring spoons
mixing bowl
spoon
cookie sheet

How To Do It

1. Put 1-1/2 cups whole wheat flour and the yeast into bowl. Mix well with fork.
2. Add salt, water, and honey and mix.
3. Add remaining wheat flour and mix.
4. Add white flour and continue mixing until dough is springy and not sticky.
5. Grease cookie sheet.
6. Divide dough into 12 pieces, each about 20 inches long. Mold into dreidel shape pretzels and using a spoon, place on cookie sheet.
7. Bake at 425 degrees Fahrenheit for 20 minutes.

Spin - A- Muffin

Serves 4

Ingredients

1 cup flour
1/2 cup quick oats
1/4 cup sugar
2 teaspoons baking powder
1/2 teaspoon salt
1 egg
1/4 cup oil
3/4 cup milk

Utensils

measuring cups
measuring spoons
2 bowls
fork
muffin pan
paper petit fours cups
tablespoon

Q. How many brothers did Judah the Maccabee have?

A. 4

Q. Which song is sung after lighting the Hanukkah candles?

A. Maoz Tzur (Rock of Ages)

How To Do It

1. Put dry ingredients: flour, oats, sugar, baking powder and salt, into bowl. Mix with fork.
2. Put egg, oil and milk into second bowl. Beat with fork till well mixed.
3. Pour milk mixture into bowl with dry ingredients. Stir till mixed, but still lumpy.
4. Line muffin pan with petit fours cups.
5. Spoon muffin mixture into muffin pan till each petit fours cup is 2/3 full.
6. Bake at 400 degrees Fahrenheit for 20 minutes.

Chocolate Cannon Balls

PARVE

Makes 20

Ingredients

1/2 lb. graham crackers
2 oz. bittersweet chocolate
2 tablespoons cocoa
1/2 cup sugar
1/4 cup wine
1/2 cup water
1/2 teaspoon rum extract
1/2 cup grated coconut

Utensils

measuring cups
measuring spoons
plastic bag with tie
wooden spoon
rolling pin
mixing bowl
tray
soup bowl
spoon
paper petit fours cups

How To Do It

1. Put the crackers into a plastic bag and tie the bag.
2. Roll the rolling pin over crackers till all the crackers are crumbled.
3. Put crumbled crackers into mixing bowl.
4. Put chocolate, cocoa, sugar, wine, water and rum extract into pot. Cook till the mixture begins to boil, constantly stirring with a wooden spoon.
5. Pour chocolate mixture into mixing bowl and mix well.
6. Put grated coconut into soup bowl.
7. Arrange the petit fours cups on a tray.
8. Shape the chocolate mixture into small balls (see illustration). Put in plate.
9. Roll the chocolate balls in the coconut and place in petit fours cups.
10. Refrigerate for 2 hours.

actual size

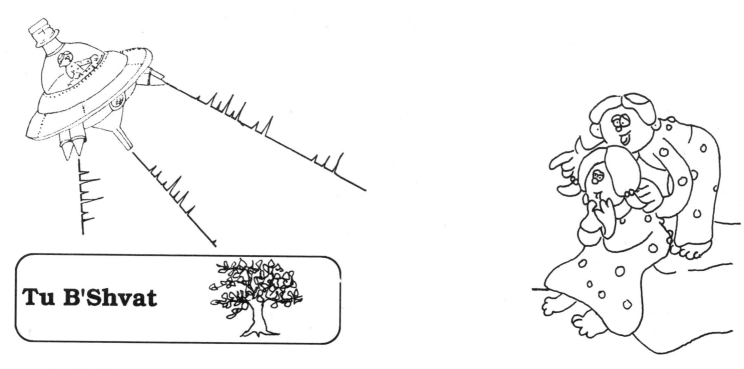

Tu B'Shvat

Tu B' Shvat is mentioned in the Mishna as the New Year for Trees. We make a point of eating a fruit that grows in Israel on this day, especially the fruit of the carob (boxer) tree.

Date: 15th of Shvat

Granola Treats

Serves 4

Ingredients

1/3 cup honey
1 teaspoon cornstarch
1 cup granola
1/3 cup peanut butter

Utensils

measuring cups
measuring spoons
pot
wooden spoon
cookie sheet
wax paper
teaspoon

Q. What holiday celebrates the "New Year of the Trees"?

A. Tu B'Shvat

How To Do It

1. Put honey, cornstarch and granola into pot. Cook on low heat till ingredients are well blended, constantly mixing with wooden spoon.
2. Remove pot from heat.
3. Add peanut butter to pot. Mix well.
4. Cover cookie sheet with wax paper.
5. Using a teaspoon, place batter on cookie sheet. Leave 3 fingers space between each cookie. Repeat till all the granola mixture is used.
6. Refrigerate for 3 hours or till firm.

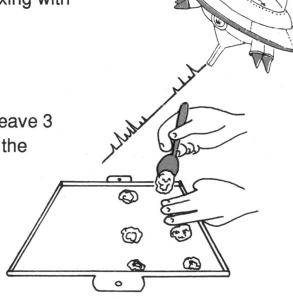

Date Delight

Ingredients

6-1/2 oz. margarine
1/2 cup sugar
2 tablespoons honey
10 oz. pitted dates
3/4 lb. rice crispies

Utensils

measuring cups
measuring spoons
pot
bowl
fork
wooden spoon
paper petit fours cups
tray

Q. Name the special fruit you eat on Tu B'Shvat?

A. Boxer

How To Do It

1. Put margarine, sugar and honey into pot.
2. Cook on low heat till margarine is melted. Remove pot from heat before mixture boils.
3. Put dates into bowl and mash with fork.
4. Add mashed dates to pot. Mix with wooden spoon.
5. Put rice crispies into bowl.
6. Add date mixture to bowl. Mix well.
7. Place petit fours cups on tray.
8. Take teaspoonful of date mixture. Shape into ball (see illustration). Put date ball into petit fours cups.
9. Repeat #8 till all date mixture is used.

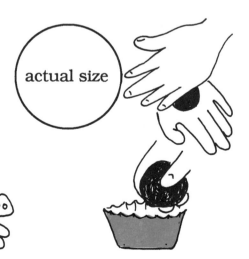

actual size

Date A Nut

PARVE

Serves 3

Ingredients

12 large pitted dates
12 large walnuts
1/4 cup coconut flakes

Utensils

measuring cups
knife
bowl
paper doily
serving platter

How To Do It

1. Cut dates lengthwise with knife, but do not cut in half.
2. Put a walnut into each date. Squeeze date closed.
3. Pour coconut into small bowl.
4. Roll stuffed dates in coconut till they are completely covered with coconut.
5. Place paper doily on serving platter.
6. Arrange dates on serving platter.

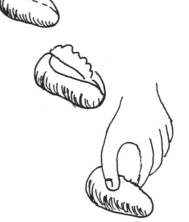

69

Fruity Jello

PARVE

Serves 4

Ingredients

1 package flavored kosher jello
1-1/2 cups water
1 cup juice from fruit cocktail
1 can fruit cocktail

Utensils

measuring cups
bowl
pot
wooden spoon
can opener
4 serving cups

How To Do It

1. Put jello into bowl.
2. Boil water in pot.
3. Add 1 cup of boiling water to bowl. Stir with wooden spoon till jello is dissolved.
4. Add canned fruit juice to bowl. Mix well.
5. Pour jello mixture into serving cups.
6. Put 2 tablespoons of fruit cocktail into each cup of jello.
7. Let cool and then refrigerate. Serve cold.

PURIM

The name Purim comes from the Persian word "Pur" which means lottery. The wicked Haman used a lottery to select the date for the destruction of the Jews in all the lands of King Ahashverosh. But Mordechai and Esther, after discovering Haman's plan, were able to turn the tables on him. The Jews were armed and went out and destroyed all those who were preparing to kill them.

Date: 14th of Adar

Basic Mitzvot:

Reading the Megillah-- Men and Women are required to listen to the reading of the Megillah on the evening of Purim, and again on the morning of Purim. The Megillah tells not only the story of Purim, but also how the Jews re-established their connection with G-d through prayer, fasting and repentence.

Seudah-- On Purim afternoon a special feast is eaten. Meat and wine are the two most important foods of this meal. Adults drink more than usual at the meal since Haman met his downfall at the feast of wine which Esther prepared for him.

Shalach Manot-- Each person sends two types of edible foods to a
friend. Children often serve as messengers, delivering
these presents.

Gifts to the Poor-- Each person gives a gift to at least two poor people.

Customs and Symbols:

Groggers-- Noisemakers that are used to drown out the name of Haman
during the reading of the Megillah.

Costumes-- Everyone gets dressed up in their favorite costume. In
many communities there are Purim parties and carnivals.

Manna Cakes

Serves 4

Ingredients

4 eggs
1/2 cup water
1/2 cup milk
1/2 teaspoon salt
1 cup matza meal
oil for frying

Utensils

measuring cups
measuring spoons
bowl
fork
frying pan
tablespoon
spatula

Q. Why do we wear costumes on Purim?
A. So we won't be able to recognize each other. This is another way of not being able to tell the difference between Mordechai and Haman.

How To Do It

1. Put eggs, water, milk and salt into bowl. Mix with fork till well blended.
2. Add matza meal to bowl. Mix with fork. Let the mixture stand for 10 minutes to thicken slightly.
3. Heat oil in frying pan.
4. Take a heaping tablespoonful of pancake mixture and carefully place it in the hot oil. Repeat till all the pancake mixture is used.
5. Fry till pancakes are brown on bottom. Turn pancakes over with spatula and fry till other side is golden brown.

Pasta and Meat Complete

 MEAT

Serves 8

Ingredients

2 quarts water
1/2 lb. spaghetti
1 onion
1 clove garlic
1/2 green pepper
3 tablespoons oil
1 teaspoon salt
1/4 teaspoon pepper
1/2 teaspoon oregano
1 lb. ground beef
1 8 oz. can tomato sauce
1 can tomato paste
1 tablespoon sugar

Utensils

measuring cups
measuring spoons
large pot
fork
colander
knife
cutting board

Q. When is Shabbat Zachor?

A. The Shabbat before Purim.

How To Do It

1. Boil 2 quarts water in pot. Place spaghetti into boiling
   water. Stir with fork. Cook spaghetti on medium heat till soft.
2. Put colander into sink. Pour spaghetti into colander to drain
   water. Rinse spaghetti with cold water. Leave spaghetti in colander.
3. Peel onions and garlic. Cut into small pieces with knife on cutting board.
4. Wash green pepper. Cut it in half. Remove seeds.
   Cut 1/2 green pepper into small pieces on cutting board.
5. Heat oil in a dry pot.

6. Add onions, green pepper, garlic, salt, pepper and oregano to pot and cook on medium flame till vegetables are soft.
7. Add beef. Constantly stir mixture with fork till beef is brown.
8. Add tomato sauce, tomato paste and sugar. Bring mixture to a boil.
9. Add spaghetti. Bring to a boil again. Stir.

Dogs in a Blanket

MEAT

Serves 6-8

Ingredients

1 package frozen pastry puff dough
3 tablespoons flour
15 hot dogs
1 egg
sesame seeds
oil for greasing

Utensils

measuring spoons
large casserole dish
rolling pin
knife
fork
small bowl
pastry brush

How To Do It

1. Take dough out of freezer to defrost.
2. Grease casserole dish.
3. Sprinkle flour on table. Roll dough with rolling pin as thin as you can without tearing dough.
4. Place hot dogs in two parallel rows on dough. Leave 3 fingers space on both sides of each hot dog.
5. Cut dough with knife on both sides of hot dogs. Wrap dough around hot dogs and pinch closed on both ends.
6. Cut each hot dog wrapped in dough into 3 small pieces. Put into casserole dish.
7. Beat egg with fork in small bowl.
8. Brush some egg on each rolled hot dog and sprinkle with sesame seeds.
9. Bake at 350 degrees Fahrenheit for 45 minutes or till dough is golden brown.

Chewy Crunch Bars

Ingredients

2 tablespoons margarine
1/2 cup brown sugar
1/2 cup light corn syrup
1/2 cup peanut butter
1 cup unsalted peanuts
1 cup corn flakes
1 cup thin chow mein noodles
6 oz. chocolate chips

Utensils

measuring cups
measuring spoons
pot
spoon
baking pan
fork

Hamantashen is the Yiddish word for "Haman's pockets" which may represent the pocketsful of money he used to bribe King Ahashverosh. In Israel they are called "oznai Haman", Haman's ears which makes fun of the Dumbo-like way he looked.

How To Do It

1. Put margarine, brown sugar, corn syrup and peanut butter into pot. Melt on low heat.
2. Add peanuts, corn flakes and chow mein noodles to pot. Mix well with spoon.
3. Put peanut mixture into baking pan. Press mixture down with fork to flatten top.
4. Put chocolate chips into pot. Melt on low heat.
5. Pour melted chocolate into baking pan. With spatula spread chocolate evenly over peanut mixture.
6. Refrigerate for 2 hours.
7. Remove baking pan from refrigerator. Cut into squares.

Chocolate Cake

PARVE

A beggar went into a restaurant on Purim, ate and drank his fill but when they brought him the bill he told the owner: "Thank you for the wonderful Purim meal." "What do you mean?" fumed the owner. "You eat, you pay!" "Take it easy," said the beggar. "I haven't any money just now but I"ll go out into the ☞

Ingredients

oil for greasing
1 cup water
1-1/2 cups flour
1-1/2 cups sugar
1/2 teaspoon baking soda
1-1/2 teaspoons baking powder
1/2 teaspoon salt
1/2 cup cocoa
1/2 cup oil
1 tablespoon instant coffee
2 teaspoons vanilla
3 eggs

Utensils

measuring cups
measuring spoons
9x9x2 inch baking pan
small pot with lid
electric mixer
mixer bowl
rubber spatula

How To Do It

1. Grease baking pan.
2. Boil water in pot. Put in bowl.
3. Put remaining ingredients into mixer bowl in order listed.
4. Beat on medium speed for 10 minutes.
5. Using spatula pour into baking pan.
6. Bake at 350 degrees Fahrenheit for 45 minutes.

Easy Brownies PARVE

Serves 15

Ingredients

3/4 cup cocoa
1/2 teaspoon baking soda
2/3 cup oil
3/4 cup water
2 cups sugar
1 teaspoon vanilla
2 eggs
1 teaspoon salt
1-1/3 cups flour

Utensils

measuring cups
measuring spoons
bowl
wooden spoon
kettle
13x11 inch baking pan

street and get the money people give to the poor today and I'll bring you all I collect." "How do I know you'll come back and pay?" mocked the owner. "O.K., so come with me," answered the beggar. "What? Go with a beggar!" exclaimed the owner. "All right, if it's beneath your dignity to be seen with me, I'll stay here and you can go and collect the money yourself."

How To Do It

1. Put cocoa, baking soda and 1/3 cup of oil into bowl. Mix well with wooden spoon.
2. Boil water in kettle.
3. Measure 1/2 cup of boiling water and add to bowl. Mix till mixture thickens.
4. Add sugar and vanilla to bowl and mix well.
5. Add remaining 1/3 cup of oil, eggs and salt to bowl. Mix well.
6. Add flour to bowl and mix well.
7. Pour cake mixture into cake pan.
8. Bake at 350 degrees Fahrenheit for 1/2 hour.

<u>Now try this:</u> *Add the following after step #6: 1 cup of chopped nuts or 2 cups of chocolate bits*

Swirls of Twirls

PARVE

Ingredients

3/4 cup margarine
1-1/2 cup sugar
3 eggs
3 cups flour
3 teaspoons baking powder
1 teaspoon salt
1 cup orange juice
1-1/2 teaspoon vanilla
red, green and yellow food coloring
oil for greasing

Utensils

measuring cups
measuring spoons
electric mixer
mixer bowl
2 mixing bowls
rubber spatula
9 inch tube pan

How To Do It

1. Put margarine and sugar into mixer bowl. Beat on medium speed till mixture is lightcolored and fluffy.
2. Add eggs, one at a time. Beat 2 minutes on medium speed after adding each egg.
3. Put flour, baking powder and salt into mixing bowl.
4. Put orange juice and vanilla into another mixing bowl.
5. Add 1/3 of flour mixture to mixer bowl. Beat 1/2 minute on medium speed. Add 1/3 of orange juice mixture to mixer bowl. Beat 1/2 minute on medium speed.
6. Repeat step number 5 another 2 times.
7. Grease the baking pan.
8. Pour 1/3 of batter into mixing bowl using spatula. Pour 1/3 of batter into second mixing bowl. Leave 1/3 of batter in mixer bowl.
9. Make each batter a different color by adding a few drops of red, green or yellow food coloring.

10. Pour the red batter into the baking pan. Pour the yellow batter on top of the red batter. Pour the green batter on top of the yellow batter.

11. Bake at 325 degrees Fahrenheit for 45 minutes. Turn the temperature to 350 degrees Fahrenheit and bake another 15 minutes.

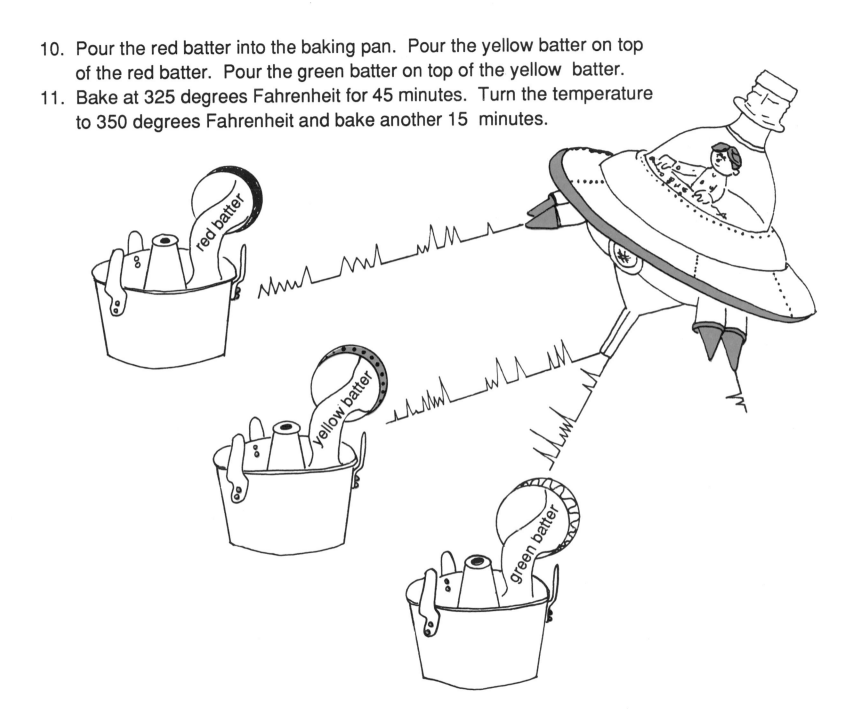

Chocolate Frosting

PARVE

Ingredients

4 oz. margarine
1 lb. confectioners sugar
2 tablespoons cocoa
2 tablespoons warm water

Utensils

measuring spoons
electric mixer
mixer bowl

Q. How many provinces did Achashverosh rule?

A. 127

Q. How many sons did Haman have?

A. 10

How To Do It

1. Put margarine and confectioners sugar into mixer bowl. Beat for 5 minutes.
2. Add cocoa to mixer bowl. Beat.
3. Add warm water and beat till mixture is well blended.

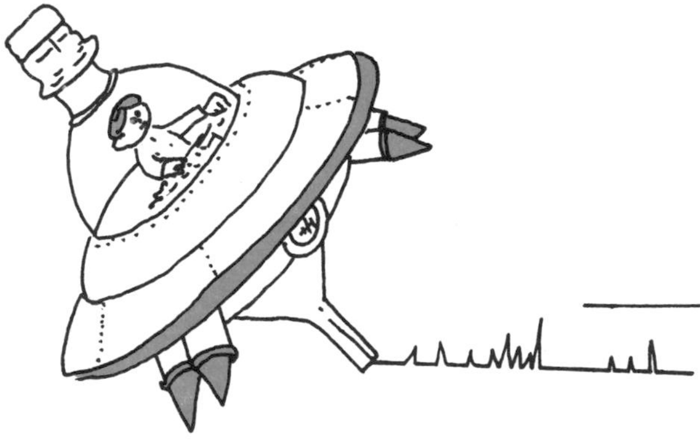

Granny's Homemade Granola

PARVE

Ingredients

6-1/2 cups rolled oats
1 cup grated coconut
1-1/4 cups wheat germ
1 cup sesame seeds
3 teaspoons cinnamon
3/4 cup brown sugar
1/3 cup honey
6 tablespoons oil
1/4 cup water

Utensils

measuring cups
measuring spoons
large bowl
small pot
wooden spoon
cookie sheet

Haman was a descendent of the Amalek nation, the first people to attack the Jews as they left Egypt.

How To Do It

1. Put dry ingredients: oats, coconut, wheat germ, sesame seeds, cinnamon and brown sugar into large bowl.
2. Put honey, oil and water in pot. Cook on low heat till honey mixture begins to boil.
3. Remove from heat.
4. Pour honey mixture over dry ingredients in bowl Mix well with wooden spoon.
5. Put granola mixture onto cookie sheet. Spread evenly.
6. Bake at 350 degrees Fahrenheit for 20 minutes.
7. Stir mixture on cookie sheet with wooden spoon.
8. Bake for another 20 minutes.

Rice Crispy Chocolate Candies DAIRY

Ingredients

4 ozs. milk chocolate
1-1/2 cups rice crispies

Utensils

small pot
wooden spoon
petit fours cups
large tray

Q. Which Hebrew month comes twice during a leap year?

A. Adar

How To Do It

1. Put chocolate into small pot and melt on low heat.
2. Remove pot from heat.
3. Add rice crispies to pot and mix well with wooden spoon.
4. Place petit fours cups on a large tray. Put a teaspoonful of mixture into each petit fours cup.
5. Refrigerate for 4 hours.

Now Try This: *Substitute any of the following for #3*

Add 1 cup rice crispies and 1/2 cup raisins.

Add 1-1/2 cups cornflakes.

Add 1-1/2 cups peanuts.

84

Chocolate Chip Cookies

Makes 25

Ingredients

1 cup margarine
1 cup brown sugar
1 cup white sugar
2 eggs
1 teaspoon vanilla
1 teaspoon baking soda
2-1/3 cups flour
8 oz. chocolate chips
1 cup chopped walnuts
oil for greasing

Utensils

measuring cups
measuring spoons
electric mixer
mixer bowl
cookie sheet

> Some eat raw vegetables at the meal to recall that when Esther went to meet the king she did not eat meat or food prepared by non-Jews.

How To Do It

1. Put margarine, brown sugar and white sugar into mixer bowl. Beat on medium speed till mixture is smooth.
2. Add eggs, vanilla, baking soda, flour, chocolate chips and walnuts to mixer bowl. Beat on medium speed till cookie mixture is well blended.
3. Grease the cookie sheet.
4. Using a teaspoon, place batter on cookie sheet. Leave 2 fingers space between each cookie.
5. Bake at 350 degrees Fahrenheit for 8-10 minutes.

Orange Peel Candies

Serves 3

Ingredients

4 oranges
1-1/2 cups sugar
1/2 cup water

Utensils

measuring cups
pot
colander
fork
cutting board
knife

How To Do It

1. Peel the oranges.
2. Put orange peels into pot. Add water to cover peels.
3. Cook peels till water boils. Turn off heat.
4. Put colander into sink. Carefully pour boiling water and orange peels into colander.
5. Repeat number 2 to 4 another 3 times. This takes the bitterness out of the orange peels.
6. Cut the orange peels into strips with knife on cutting board.
7. Measure 2 cups of orange peel strips. Put into pot.
8. Add sugar and water to pot.
9. Cook till water boils. Lower heat. Cook for 35 minutes.
10. Pour water and orange peel strips into the colander.
11. Wet cutting board under water faucet.
12. Put orange peel strips onto wet cutting board.
13. Separate strips with fork. Leave the strips on cutting board to dry.

PESACH

Pesach, or Passover, as the festival is called in English, recalls the exodus of the Jews from Egypt. Over 3300 years ago G-d sent Moshe and his brother, Aaron, to convince Pharaoh, the king of Egypt, to free the Jews from slavery. Only after suffering the effects of the 10 Plagues did Pharaoh agree to let the Jews go.

This exodus from Egypt marks the birth of the Jews as a free people.

Date: 15th of Nissan

Basic Mitzvot:

Eating Matza -- No leavened foods may be eaten during all of Pesach. Matza is a mixture of flour and water which have come into contact with each other for <u>no</u> longer than 18 minutes. Matza must be eaten on the first night of Pesach.

Biur Hametz -- On the night before Pesach we search the house for any leavened foods. On the following morning we burn whatever leavened foods remain.

The Seder -- The Seder comprises a number of mitzvot which are vital to the celebration of Pesach.

    1. Drinking the 4 Cups of Wine
    2. Eating the Matza and other items of the Seder Plate
    3. Telling the Story of Pesach

Counting of the Omer -- Beginning with the second night of Pesach and every night after, we count the days for a period of 7 full weeks. On the 50th day is Shavuot.

Customs and Symbols:

Matza Shmurah -- Wheat which is specially watched to make sure it has not come into contact with water from the time of reaping.

Fast of the First Born -- Since G-d spared the first-born sons of the Jews when the 10th Plague struck Egypt, first-born sons fast on the morning before Passover. It is permissible to break the fast by taking part in a religious feast (brit or wedding), or by completing a tractate of the Talmud.

Maot Chittim -- Charitable funds collected so that poor people can buy matza.

Don't Passover Rolls

Makes 10

Ingredients

1/2 cup oil
1 cup water
2 cups matzo meal
1 teaspoon salt
1 tablespoon sugar
4 eggs
oil for greasing

Utensils

measuring cups
measuring spoons
pot
spoon
cookie sheet

Q. Why is the matza called "the poor man's bread"?

A. Just like a poor person, we break the matza and leave some for later.

Q. Why do we spill out a little wine when reciting the section about The Plagues?

A. To show that the death of even our enemies lessens our joy.

How To Do It

1. Preheat oven to 350 degrees Fahrenheit.
2. Pour oil and water into pot. Bring to a boil. Remove pot from heat.
3. Add matza meal, salt and sugar to pot. Mix well with spoon.
4. Beat each egg in bowl and add them one at a time to pot. Mix well after each addition.
5. Let mixture stand at room temperature for 10 minutes.
6. Grease cookie sheet.
7. Shape mixture into balls (see illustration) and place on cookie sheet.
8. Bake about 45 minutes or till golden brown.

Now Try This: *After step #7, wet index finger with water and make a hole in the center of each ball. Now you've turned Passover rolls into Passover bagels.*

actual size

Kneidel Clouds

Serves 9

Ingredients

1/3 cup margarine
4 eggs
1 teaspoon salt
1/2 cup soda water (seltzer)
1 cup unsalted matza meal
1-1/2 quarts water

Utensils

measuring spoons
measuring cups
frying pan
bowl
fork
spoon
2 quart pot with lid
slotted spoon

Exactly 400 years to the day passed from the birth of Isaac on the 15th of Nissan to the Exodus on Passover. (Sifsay Chachomim)

How To Do It

1. Melt margarine in frying pan. Cool for a few minutes.
2. Put eggs into bowl. Beat eggs with fork.
3. Add salt, soda water, melted margarine and matza meal to bowl. Mix well with spoon.
4. Refrigerate matza meal mixture about one hour.
5. Boil water in covered pot.
6. Roll matza meal mixture into balls (see illustration).
7. Put each kneidel on slotted spoon, one at a time, and place into boiling water. (If your hands get too sticky wet them.)
8. Boil gently for 20 minutes in covered pot. Remove pot from heat.
9. Remove kneidels from pot with slotted spoon.

actual size

Potato Kneidel PARVE

Serves 5

Ingredients

5 medium potatoes
2 eggs
2/3 cup potato flour
2 teaspoons salt
6 cups water

Utensils

measuring cups
measuring spoons
potato peeler
small bowl
mixing bowl
2 quart pot with lid
fork
slotted spoon
bowl
mixing bowl

actual size

How To Do It

1. Peel and wash potatoes.
2. Put potatoes into pot. Add water to cover potatoes. Cover pot.
3. Cook potatoes for 20 minutes or till soft enough to pierce with fork.
4. Remove potatoes from pot with slotted spoon and put into bowl.
5. Mash well with fork. Measure 2 cups of potato mixture and put into mixing bowl.
6. Put eggs into small bowl. Beat with fork.
7. Add eggs, potato flour and salt to mixing bowl. Mix well. Make sure there are no lumps of potato in mixture.
8. Put water into pot. Add remaining salt to pot. Cover pot.
9. Boil water.
10. Roll potato mixture into balls (see illustration). If your hands get too sticky wet them.
11. Put each kneidel on slotted spoon, one at a time, and place into boiling water.
12. Cook gently for 20 minutes. Remove pot from heat.
13. Remove kneidels from pot with slotted spoon.

Charoset - The Mortar You Love to Eat

Ingredients

2 large apples
1/2 cup chopped almonds
1/4 cup chopped walnuts
1/2 teaspoon cinnamon
1/3 cup sweet red wine

Utensils

measuring cups
measuring spoons
grater
knife
bowl
spoon

> We dip the karpas — symbolizing the 600,000 Jews who worked so hard—into the salt water to remind us of the 600,000 Jews who crossed the Red Sea.
>
> The charoset reminds us of the mortar used by the Jews in Egypt to build Egyptian cities.

How To Do It

1. Wash and peel apples.
2. Grate apples with fine grater into bowl. Discard cores.
3. Add almonds, walnuts and cinnamon to bowl. Mix well with fork.
4. Add wine slowly till mixture forms a paste.

Possible additions: *chopped dates, dried fruits*

92

Carrot - Top Kugel

Serves 8

The day Jacob dressed up as Esav in order to get the Blessing of the First Born from his father was Passover. (Rashi)

Ingredients

1 teaspoon oil for greasing
2 cans of carrots (32 oz.)
4 eggs
1/4 cup brown sugar
1/4 cup white sugar
1/2 cup soft margarine
1 tablespoon almond flavoring
1 cup matza meal
2 teaspoons baking powder

Utensils

measuring cups
measuring spoons
fork
mixing bowl
1 quart casserole dish

How To Do It

1. Grease casserole dish.
2. Drain liquid from cans of carrots.
3. Put carrots in bowl. Mash carrots with fork.
4. Add remaining ingredients to bowl. Mix well.
5. Pour carrot mixture into casserole dish and press down with fork.
6. Bake at 350 degrees Fahrenheit for 1 hour or till brown

Knish Knosh Burekas

PARVE

Serves 2-3

Ingredients

4 potatoes
2 small onions
6 tablespoons oil for frying
1/4 teaspoon salt
1/4 teaspoon pepper
4 matzas
4 eggs

Utensils

measuring spoons
potato peeler
knife
cutting board
pot with lid
fork
slotted spoon
bowl
frying pan
spatula
paper towel
plate

A man came to the rabbi to complain about the mice in his kitchen. "They've eaten everything up," he cried. "What am I to do?" "Take some Afikoman crumbs," advised the rabbi, "and put them in front of the mouse holes. Everyone knows that you're not allowed to eat anything after the Afikoman, so the mice will leave the rest of your food alone." The man blinked twice and then asked, "But rabbi, how do the mice know such a law?" The rabbi smiled and answered,"Don't be silly. Why, just last week the mice ate the Passover volume of my Talmud!"

How To Do It

1. Peel and wash potatoes.
2. Cut potatoes into quarters with knife on cutting board.
3. Put potatoes into pot. Add water to cover potatoes. Put lid on pot.
4. Boil for 20 minutes or till soft enough to pierce with fork.
5. Take potatoes out of pot with slotted spoon and put into bowl. Mash well with fork.
6. Peel onions. Cut into small pieces with knife on cutting board.
7. Heat 3 tablespoons of oil in frying pan.
8. Fry onions till golden brown. Remove from heat.
9. Add onions, salt and pepper to bowl. Mix well with fork.

10. Hold matza under water faucet till wet and soft.
11. Cut matza into four equal quarters.
12. Put potato filling on each quarter.
13. Fold matza to make a triangle shape.
14. Repeat steps 10-13 for each matza.
15. Put eggs into bowl. Beat with fork.
16. Dip each triangle into beaten egg.
17. Heat remaining 3 tablespoons of oil in frying pan.
18. Fry burekas till bottom is golden brown. With spatula turn burekas over and fry till other side is golden brown.
19. Put paper towel on plate. With spatula, remove burekas from frying pan. Place on paper towel to drain till ready to serve.

Q. What do we do on the Fast of the Firstborn Son?

A. We conclude a tractate of the Talmud so we can break our fast.

Q. What does "Bittul Chametz" mean?

A. All the chametz in my possession is worth nothing (dust and ashes).

Chocolate Matza Canapes

DAIRY

Serves 1

Ingredients

1 matza
3 oz. cream cheese
3 tablespoons cherry or apricot jam
3 oz. semisweet chocolate

Utensils

measuring spoons
wax paper
plate
knife
double boiler
rubber spatula

How To Do It

1. Place wax paper on plate. Set aside.
2. Break matza into 4 pieces.
3. Using a knife spread cream cheese on 2 of the pieces. Spread jam on remaining 2 pieces.
4. Put pieces of matza together in little jam and cheese sandwiches.
5. Melt chocolate in top of double boiler over hot, but not boiling, water. Remove from heat. You can also put the chocolate into a glass bowl and melt it in a microwave oven, if you have one.
6. Using a knife, spread melted chocolate over top and sides of each sandwich. Use rubber spatula to scrape chocolate from pot.
7. Place sandwiches on wax paper.
8. Refrigerate till ready to serve.

Mish Mosh Matza

Serves 4

Ingredients

4 cups water
5 matzas
3 tablespoons butter
1/2 lb. cottage cheese
1/2 teaspoon salt
1 teaspoon sugar

Utensils

measuring cups
measuring spoons
1-1/2 quart pot
colander
fork
bowl
frying pan
large spoon

Q. Why is the Shabbat before Passover called "Shabbat Ha'Gadol"?

A. 1. The Jews in Egypt were commanded to take a lamb for the Passover sacrifice. In Egypt the lamb was considered to be a god. It was a great day for the Jews because the Egyptians were too scared to attack us even though we sacrificed their god. 2. The reading from the Prophets (Haftorah) in the Synagogue on Shabbat HaGadol talks of the Great Day when the Mashiach will come.

How To Do It

1. Boil 4 cups of water in pot.
2. Remove pot from heat.
3. Break matzas into small pieces.
4. Put matza pieces into pot. Let stand for 10 minutes.
5. Put colander into sink. Pour matza into colander to drain.
6. Press extra water out of matzas with fork.
7. Put matzas into bowl.
8. Melt butter in frying pan. Add to bowl.
9. Add cottage cheese, salt and sugar to bowl. Mix well with spoon. Serve immediately.

This tastes very similar to noodles and cottage cheese.

"Say Cheese!" Blintzes DAIRY

Serves 2

Ingredients

4 tablespoons butter
2 cups cottage cheese
4 eggs
2 tablespoons sour cream
2 tablespoons sugar
2 matzas
1/4 cup oil for frying

Utensils

measuring cups
measuring spoons
frying pan
bowl
fork
knife
spatula

How To Do It

1. Melt butter in frying pan. Remove frying pan from heat.
2. Pour butter into bowl.
3. Add cheese, 2 eggs, sour cream and sugar to bowl. Beat well with fork.
4. Divide blintze filling into four parts.
5. Hold matza under water faucet till wet and soft. Cut matza in half with knife. Repeat for second matza.
6. Put one half of filling on each matza. Fold matza over to cover filling.
7. Put remaining 2 eggs into bowl. Beat with fork.
8. Dip both sides of blintzes into beaten eggs.
9. Heat oil in frying pan.
10. Fry till bottom is golden brown. With spatula turn blintzes over and fry till other side is golden brown.

Serve the blintzes with your favorite topping such as sour cream, sugar, fruit cocktail, chocolate syrup, etc.

Matza Pizza Treatsa

DAIRY

Serves 4

Ingredients

6 matzas
4 eggs
1/4 teaspoon salt
1/4 teaspoon pepper
1 cup tomato sauce
9 slices of yellow cheese
oil for greasing

Utensils

measuring cups
measuring spoons
mixing bowl
fork
small bowl
9 inch baking pan

Q. What special charity do the Jews give before Passover?

A. Ma'ot Chitim - money given to the poor to buy matza for Passover.

How To Do It

1. Preheat oven to 350 degrees Fahrenheit.
2. Break matzas into small pieces. Put into mixing bowl.
3. Add tap water and soak matzas for two minutes to soften.
4. Drain water from mixing bowl.
5. Beat eggs in small bowl with fork. Add to mixing bowl.
6. Add salt and pepper to mixing bowl.
7. Grease pan.
8. Pour matza mixture into baking pan. Bake for about 10 minutes. Remove from oven.
9. Add tomato sauce and cheese to baking pan.
10. Bake the pizza ten more minutes or til cheese bubbles and melts.

Matza Brei

DAINY

Serves 4

Ingredients

5 matzas
3 eggs
1/4 cup milk
1 teaspoon salt
3 tablespoons butter

Utensils

measuring cups
measuring spoons
bowl
spoon
frying pan
wooden spoon

How To Do It

1. Break matzas into small pieces. Put into bowl.
2. Add tap water and soak matzas for two minutes to soften.
3. Squeeze matzas to remove water. Empty remaining water from bowl. Place squeezed matzas back into bowl.
4. Add eggs, milk and salt to bowl. Mix well with spoon.
5. Melt butter in frying pan.
6. With spatula gently place matza mixture into frying pan. Fry till bottom is golden brown. Turn matza brei over with spatula till other side is golden brown.

You can eat the matza brei with syrup, jam or sugar.

Two poor people, a Jew and a non-Jew, decided to go into the town of Bendin in Poland to partake of the Seder. "Don't forget," said the Jew to the non-Jew, "tonight is the night every household is open to us. We need but sit and wait to be served." "Sounds great to me," said the non-Jew. "Let's meet back here later and exchange experiences," added the Jew and off they went.

After midnight the Jew returned only to see his friend angrily pacing up and down. "What happened?," he asked. "Happened?" echoed the non-jew. "Why, I've been waiting here for hours. I found a wonderful home and they let me in. But did they start eating? No. They talked and talked and then talked some more. Finally, when they decided to eat what do you think they served? I'll tell you! Horseradish! I took one taste and ran out like a bullet."

Jelly Roll

PARVE

Ingredients

6 eggs
1 cup sugar
1/2 cup cake meal
1/2 cup potato starch
1 teaspoon salt
jam to cover cake

Utensils

measuring cups
measuring spoons
electric mixer
mixer bowl
spatula
dish towel
15 x 10-1/2 jelly roll pan
wax paper
knife

The Jew laughed. "Oh, my friend," he said, "had you only remained for the bitter part of the evening, you would have so enjoyed the sweet part that came later."

How To Do It

1. Put eggs and sugar into bowl. Beat on medium speed for 15 minutes.
2. Using a spatula, gently fold in cake meal, potato starch and salt.
3. Spread dish towel on table. Sprinkle sugar onto dish towel.
4. Line jelly roll pan with wax paper.
5. Spread batter on wax paper.
6. Bake at 350 degrees Fahrenheit for 20 minutes.
7. Remove pan from oven and immediately turn the pan upside down onto the dish towel.
8. Quickly and carefully remove wax paper.
9. Immediately spread jam on cake with knife.
10. Roll up in jelly roll shape.

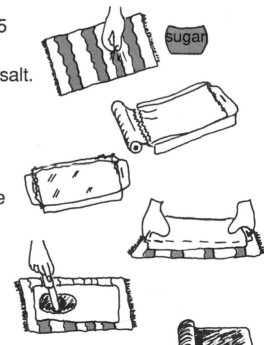

sugar

Chocolate Drops PARVE

The z'roah—the shank bone—reminds us of the Passover lamb sacrificed in Egypt.

Ingredients

2 eggs
1 cup sugar
2 cups ground nuts
1/4 teaspoon salt
1 tablespoon cocoa

Utensils

measuring cups
measuring spoons
electric mixer
mixer bowl
cookie sheet
teaspoon

How To Do It

1. Put eggs, sugar, nuts, salt, and cocoa into mixer bowl. Beat on medium speed to make a smooth batter.
2. Grease cookie sheet.
3. Using a teaspoon, place batter on cookie sheet. Leave 2 fingers space between each cookie.
4. Bake at 350 degrees Fahrenheit for 8-10 minutes.

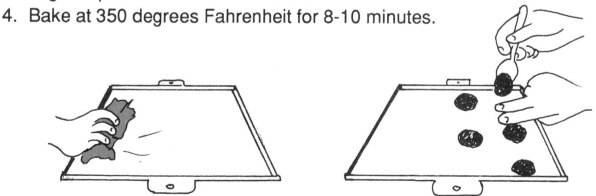

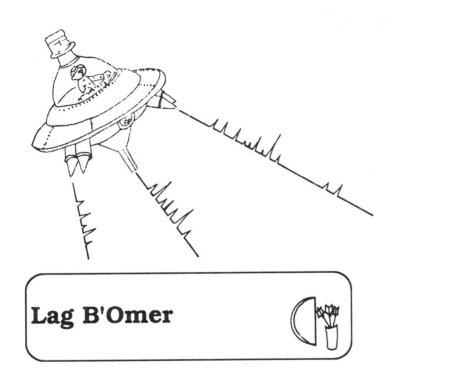

Lag B'Omer

During the 49 days between Pesach and Shavuot, called the Counting of the Omer, public celebrations are not permitted. This is because over 20,000 students of Rabbi Akiva died during this period. However, on Lag B'Omer, the 33rd day of the Counting of the Omer, the plague finally subsided. This day is therefore celebrated as a semi-holiday when weddings and bar mitzvahs are permitted.

Date: 18th of Iyar

Phony French Fries

Serves 6-8

Ingredients

8 medium potatoes
8 tablespoons oil
1 teaspoon salt

Utensils

measuring spoons
potato peeler
knife
cutting board
bowl
fork
9x11 inch baking pan

How To Do It

1. Peel potatoes with potato peeler.
2. Cut each potato into 8 wedges with knife on cutting board.
3. Put oil and salt into bowl.
4. Add 4 potato wedges to bowl.
5. Stir potatoes with fork to coat with oil. Put potatoes into baking pan.
6. Repeat # 4 and #5 till all potato wedges are coated.
7. Bake at 450 degrees Fahrenheit for 1/2 hour or till edges of potatoes are crisp.

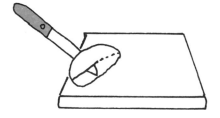

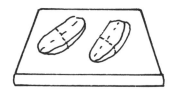

Mc' Burger

MEAT

Serves 4

Ingredients

2 lb. chopped meat
1 medium onion
1 small apple
2 tablespoons matza meal
1/2 teaspoon pepper
1 tablespoon chicken soup powder
2 teaspoons salt
1/4 teaspoon garlic salt
1/2 cup cold water
2 tablespoons ketchup
oil for frying

Utensils

measuring cups
measuring spoons
grater
knife
cutting board
spatula
frying pan
fork

Q. Which cities did the Jews build in Egypt?

A. Pithom and Ramses

Q. What is the name of the historical treaty between Jimmy Carter, Menachem Begin and Anwar Sadat?

A. The Camp David Accords

Q. Which of Jerusalem's gates is named after a Jewish king?

A. Herod's Gate

How To Do It

1. Put meat into bowl.
2. Peel onion and apple.
3. Grate onion and apple on fine grater. Add to bowl.
4. Add matza meal, pepper, soup powder, salt, garlic salt, water and ketchup to bowl. Mix well with fork.
5. Heat oil in frying pan.
6. Shape meat mixture into patties. With spatula gently put patties into oil. Fry till bottom is brown. Turn patties over and fry till other side is brown.

YOM HA'ATZMAUT

Israel Independence Day marks the reestablishment of the State of Israel in 1948. In Israel, Yom Ha'atzmaut is celebrated with special prayers, parades, fireworks, music festivals, a Bible quiz, and family barbecues.

Date: 5th of Iyar

Yom Yerushalayim

Jerusalem day is an Israeli national holiday that celebrates the anniversary of Jerusalem's reunification after the Six Day War in 1967. The Western Wall (The Kotel) and the Temple Mount returned to Jewish control for the first time since 70 C.E.

Date: 28th of Iyar

Pickled Picnic Pickles

Serves 3-4

Ingredients

4 cucumbers
2 cups water
2 cloves garlic
1 cup vinegar
3 bayleaves
8 peppercorns
1/2 teaspoon salt
1 teaspoon sugar

Utensils

measuring cups
measuring spoons
knife
cutting board
medium size pot
large glass jar with lid

Q. What is the name of the 5 year program that allows boys in Israel to learn in a yeshiva and do their army service?

A. Hesder

Q. Who ruled Palestine before the British?

A. The Turks

Q. What is the most famous Israeli weapon?

A. The Uzi

How To Do It

1. Wash cucumbers. Slice cucumbers into circles with knife on cutting board. Put cut cucumbers into glass jar.
2. Boil water in pot. Remove pot from heat.
3. Peel garlic and cut into small pieces on cutting board. Put into pot.
4. Add vinegar, bayleaves, peppercorns, salt and sugar to pot. Cook till vinegar mixture begins to boil. Remove from heat.
5. Pour vinegar mixture over cucumbers.
6. Close jar. Let jar stand at room temperature for 24 hours.
7. Refrigerate.

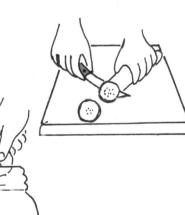

Salad On Parade

Serves 4

Ingredients

1 large can corn
1 sour pickle
1/2 red pepper
1/2 small onion
1 tablespoon lemon juice

Utensils

measuring spoons
can opener
cutting board
knife
bowl
fork

Q. Which document, in 1914, promised the Jews their own homeland?

A. The Balfour Declaration

Q. What is the name of the elite fighting force of the Hagganah?

A. The Plamach

Q. What was the name of the currency used by Israel before the Shekel?

A. The Lira

How To Do It

1. Drain liquid from can of corn.
2. Cut pickle into small pieces with knife on cutting board.
3. Wash red pepper. Cut in half. Remove seeds. Cut 1/2 red pepper into small pieces on cutting board.
4. Peel onion. Cut into small pieces on cutting board.
5. Put the corn, pickle, pepper and onion into bowl.
6. Add lemon juice to bowl. Mix well with fork.

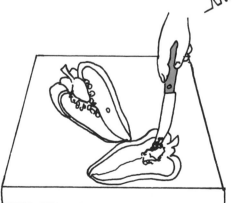

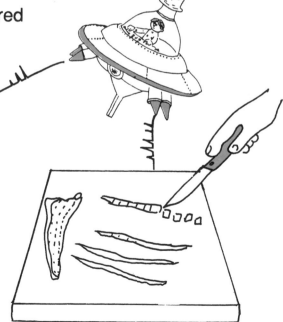

A Toast From Jerusalem

Serves 2

Ingredients

2 eggs
2/3 cups milk
1 teaspoon vanilla
1/2 teaspoon salt
1 tablespoon sugar
3 slices white bread
oil for frying

Utensils

measuring cups
measuring spoons
bowl
fork
frying pan
spatula

Q. When was the Second Temple destroyed?

A. 70 C.E.

Q. What are the colors of the Israeli flag?

A. Blue and white

Q. What type of missile helped protect Israel during the Gulf War?

A. The Patriot Missile

How To Do It

1. Beat eggs in bowl with fork.
2. Add milk, vanilla, salt and sugar to bowl.
3. Heat oil in frying pan.
4. Dip each slice of bread into egg mixture. Gently place into frying pan, one at a time. Fry till bread turns brown on bottom. Turn bread over with spatula and fry till other side is brown.
5. Use jam or syrup for topping.

Shavuot

On Shavuot G-d revealed to the Children of Israel the Ten Commandments as they gathered at the foot of Mount Sinai. It is on this holiday that the Jewish People accepted the Torah for themselves and all future generations.

Date: 6th of Sivan

Customs and Symbols:

Tikun Lail Shavuot -- All-night study of different sections of the Torah and Talmud.

Book of Ruth -- Ruth, a Moabite woman, insists on following Naomi, her mother-in-law, back to Israel and into the world of Judaism. Ruth becomes the great grandmother of King David. Many of the laws of conversion to Judaism are derived from the Book of Ruth.

Dairy Foods -- We eat at least one dairy meal on Shavuot.

Decorations -- We decorate our homes and synagogues with grass and flowers to remind us of the foothills of Mount Sinai.

Onion Soup

Serves 6

Q. What does the word "Shavuot" mean?

A. Weeks or promises

Ingredients

5 large onions
4 tablespoons flour
6 cups water
1 teaspoon salt
1/4 teaspoon pepper
2 parve boullion cubes
1/2 cup grated cheese
4 tablespoons butter for frying

Utensils

measuring cups
measuring spoons
knife
cutting board
large pot
wooden spoon
6 soup bowls
ladel

How To Do It

1. Peel and cut onions into small pieces with knife on cutting board.
2. Heat butter in pot.
3. Fry onions for 10 minutes or till soft but not brown. Mix well with wooden spoon.
4. Add flour to pot. Mix well with wooden spoon.
5. Slowly add 1 cup of water to pot, constantly mixing well with wooden spoon.
6. Add salt, pepper, boullion cube and remaining 5 cups of water to pot.
7. Continue to cook soup on medium heat for an additional 1/2 hour.
8. Remove pot from heat.
9. Put 1 tablespoonful of cheese into each soup bowl.
10. Using ladel, carefully spoon hot soup into bowls.

Cheese Dip

DAIRY

Ingredients

1 small spring onion
8 oz. cream cheese
2 cups sour cream
1/2 teaspoon paprika
1 teaspoon salt
1/4 teaspoon black pepper
1/2 teaspoon garlic salt
4 carrots
2 cucumbers
3 celery stalks
6 mushrooms
4 radishes

Utensils

measuring cups
measuring spoons
knife
cutting board
bowl
fork
serving bowl
tray

Q. Why do we stay up all night on Shavuot?

A. To correct the mistake of those who slept the night they received the Torah and forced G-d to wake them.

How To Do It

1. Peel onion. Cut onion into small pieces with knife on cutting board. Put 1 tablespoon of onion into bowl.
2. Add cream cheese, sour cream, paprika, salt, black pepper and garlic salt to bowl.
3. Mix all ingredients together with fork till well blended.
4. Put cheese dip into serving bowl.
5. Refrigerate cheese dip for three hours.
6. Wash carrots, cucumbers, celery, mushrooms and radishes.
7. Cut carrots, cucumbers and celery lengthwise into 4 pieces on cutting board.
8. Cut mushrooms and radishes in half on cutting board.
9. Put cheese dip in center of tray.
10. Arrange cut carrots, cucumbers, celery, mushrooms and radishes on tray.

Pita Pizza

DAIRY

Serves 2

Ingredients

1 pita
8 frozen broccoli spears
3 tablespoons mayonnaise
4 slices yellow cheese

Utensils

measuring spoons
knife
toaster oven pan
toaster oven

Shavuot marked the beginning of the fruit harvest when Jews brought their first ripe fruits to the Temple as a thanksgiving offering.

Shavuot also means "promises". On this day G-d promised the Jewish People they would always be His chosen people, and the Jewish People promised they would never leave G-d for an idol.

How To Do It

1. Cut pita open completely with knife.
2. Cut each pita piece in half so that you have 4 pieces of pita.
3. Place 2 broccoli spears on each pita.
4. Put 3/4 of a tablespoon of mayonnaise on each broccoli spear.
5. Put 1 slice of cheese on each pita.
6. Place pita slices on toaster oven pan.
7. Broil in toaster oven till bubbly and lightly browned.

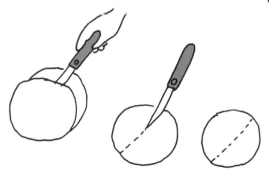

Round and Round We Go

Serves 6

Ingredients

6 medium potatoes
2 large onions
1 teaspoon salt
1/2 teaspoon pepper
1 egg
paprika for sprinkling
oil for frying

Utensils

measuring cups
measuring spoons
potato peeler
cutting board
mixing bowl
bowl
knife
large pot
frying pan
colander
fork
plate
cookie sheet

The wise men of Chelm decided to build a model of Mount Sinai for the children to see on Shavuot. "There's a mountain only a mile away," said Reb Kitzel, "let's take some stones from the mountain and bring them here so we can build our own Mount Sinai." Everyone clapped. And off they went. For days they lugged the rocks to the edge of town. Finally, just before they were finished building a small Mount Sinai, Reb Kitzel had another 🖎

How To Do It

1. Peel and wash potatoes.
2. Cut potatoes into quarters with knife on cutting board.
3. Put potatoes into pot. Add enough water to cover potatoes. Boil in covered pot for 20 minutes or till soft enough to pierce with fork.
4. Put colander into sink. Pour potatoes into colander to drain.
5. Put potatoes into bowl.
6. Peel onions and cut into small pieces with knife on cutting board.
7. Heat oil in frying pan.
8. Fry onions in frying pan till golden brown. Remove frying pan from heat.
9. Beat eggs in small bowl.

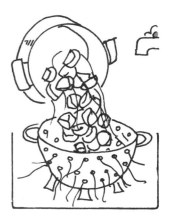

10. Mash potatoes well with fork.
11. Add onions, salt, pepper and eggs to bowl. Mix well.
12. Shape potato mixture into balls (see illustration). Put potato balls on cookie sheet.
13. Sprinkle paprika on potato balls.
14. Bake at 400 degrees Fahrenheit for 45 minutes or till balls are golden brown.

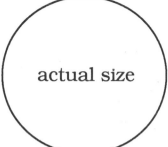

actual size

thought. "Silly us," he said out loud, wiping the sweat from his face. "Why didn't we just roll the rocks down that mountain to our town." "It's not too late," answered Reb Shiya, " we haven't finished our Mount Sinai yet. Let's bring the rocks back up the mountain and roll them down." Everyone clapped. And indeed, once they dragged the rocks back up the mountain, rolling them down was much, much easier.

Cottage Cheese Patties

Serves 4

We eat milk products on Shavuot to remind us that the Land of Israel is flowing with milk and honey.

We eat milk products on Shavuot to remind us that when we heard the laws of kashrut we could no longer use our cooking utensils and had to eat only natural foods.

Ingredients

16 oz. cottage cheese
2 eggs
1 cup corn flakes crumbs
oil for frying

Utensils

measuring cups
mixing bowl
fork
frying pan
spatula

How To Do It

1. Put cottage cheese, eggs and corn flakes crumbs into bowl. Mix well with fork.
2. Refrigerate mixture for 2 hours.
3. Heat oil in frying pan till hot.
4. Shape cottage cheese mixture into patties with hands. Put each patty on a spatula and gently place into hot oil. Fry till bottom is well browned. Turn patties over with spatula and continue frying till other side is golden brown.

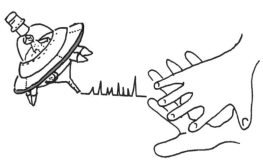

116

Ten Tuna Patties

Ingredients

2 6-1/2 oz. cans of tuna
3 eggs
1/2 cup bread crumbs
1/2 teaspoon salt
1/4 teaspoon pepper
1/4 teaspoon garlic powder
oil for frying

Utensils

measuring cups
measuring spoons
can opener
bowl
spoon
frying pan
spatula
paper towel
plate

Q. What are the 7 types of foods that make up the "first fruits" of Israel?

A. Barley, wheat, figs, grapes, pomegranates, olives and honey

How To Do It

1. Drain liquid from can of tuna.
2. Put tuna into bowl. Add eggs, bread crumbs, salt, pepper, and garlic powder to bowl. Mix well with spoon.
3. Heat oil in frying pan.
4. Shape tuna mixture into patties. Using a spatula, gently put patties into oil. Fry till bottom is brown. Turn patties over and fry till other side is brown.
5. Put paper towel on plate. Remove patties from frying pan with spatula. Place on paper towel to drain till ready to serve.

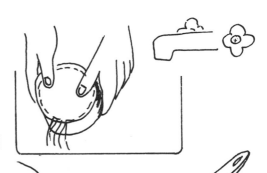

117

Hooray! Souffle!

Serves 6

Shavuot is called "Atzeret" because this holiday concludes our journey toward becoming The Jewish People, which began on Pesach.

Ingredients

oil for greasing
8 oz cottage cheese
1/2 cup sour cream
2 eggs
1 teaspoon vanilla
3 tablespoons flour
3 tablespoons sugar
3 tablespoons corn meal
6 tablespoons cherry pie filling

Utensils

measuring cups
measuring spoons
8 inch squre baking pan
mixing bowl
fork

How To Do It

1. Preheat oven to 350 degrees Fahrenheit.
2. Grease baking pan.
3. Put cottage cheese, sour cream, eggs, vanilla, flour, sugar and corn meal into bowl. Mix well with fork.
5. Pour cheese mixture into baking pan.
6. Bake for 30 minutes.
7. Top each serving with 1 tablespoon of cherry pie filling.

Strawberries and Cream

DAIRY

Serves 3

Ingredients

2 cups fresh strawberries
1/2 cup sugar
2 cups sour cream

Utensils

measuring cups
colander
knife
cutting board
bowl
spoon
3 serving cups

A young orthodox woman was being honored by her fellow workers. They couldn't help but notice she wasn't eating. "Is the food OK?" one of the workers asked. "Oh, it's just that I'm on a diet," she answered. "Since when" persisted the co-worker. "Since 2,000 years ago," came the immediate reply.

How To Do It

1. Remove stems from strawberries.
2. Put colander into sink.
3. Put strawberries into colander and wash gently with cold water.
4. Cut each strawberry into small pieces with knife on cutting board. Put into bowl.
5. Add sugar to bowl and mix gently with spoon.
6. Pour sour cream on strawberries. Mix gently.
7. Spoon strawberries into serving cups.
8. Refrigerate and serve cold.

Chocolate Cheese Cake

Ingredients

1/3 cup butter
1-1/2 cups graham cracker crumbs
1-1/4 cups sugar
16 oz. cream cheese
1/2 cup cocoa
2 teaspoons vanilla extract
2 eggs
1 cup semi-sweet chocolate chips
1 cup sour cream

Utensils

measuring cups
measuring spoons
small pot
bowl
fork
9 inch springform pan
electric mixer
mixer bowl

> The Midrash explains the custom of decorating our homes with flowers as follows: A king was about to plant a field but first he called in his servants to destroy all the thorns that had grown in the field. Suddenly, among the thorns, the king saw a beautiful flower. The king was so overwhelmed by the beauty of this flower that he declared: "For the sake of this one flower I leave this field as it is." So too, in this world. For the sake of the Torah the entire world is saved.

How To Do It

1. Melt butter in small pot.
2. Put graham cracker crumbs, 1/3 cup sugar, and melted butter into bowl. Mix well with fork.
3. Press mixture onto bottom of springform pan. Set aside.
4. Preheat oven to 375 degrees Fahrenheit.
5. Put cream cheese, 3/4 cup sugar, cocoa and 1 teaspoon vanilla into mixer bowl. Beat on medium speed until mixture is light and fluffy.
6. Add eggs. Beat till smooth.
7. Add chocolate chips and mix.
8. Pour mixture into springform pan that was set aside. Bake 20 minutes.

9. Remove from oven, cool 15 minutes. Increase oven temperature to 425 degrees Fahrenheit.

10. Mix sour cream, remaining sugar and 1 teaspoon vanilla. Stir with fork till smooth.

11. Spread evenly over baked filling. Bake 10 minutes.

12. Cool cake. Refrigerate several hours or overnight.

Creamy Fruit Salad

DAIRY

Serves 8

Ingredients

1 can mandarin orange segments
1 can pineapple chunks
1 cup green seedless grapes
4 bananas
8 oz. sour cream
2 tablespoons sugar
1 cup flaked coconut
8 maraschino cherries

Utensils

measuring cups
measuring spoons
can opener
mixing bowl
cutting board
knife
spoon
8 dessert dishes

How To Do It

1. Drain liquid from cans of orange segments and pineapple chunks. Put fruits into bowl.
2. Wash grapes. Add to bowl.
3. Peel and slice bananas with knife on cutting board. Add slices to bowl.
4. Add sour cream, sugar and coconut to bowl. Mix gently with spoon.
5. Refrigerate for 4 hours.
6. Spoon fruit and cream salad into dessert dishes. Put cherry on top of each.

Sunshine Soda

Serves 6-8

Ingredients

1 can frozen orange juice concentrate
4 cups lemon lime soda
1 tablespoon honey
1 cup water
6 ice cubes

Utensils

measuring cups
measuring spoons
mixing bowl
spoon

How To Do It

1. Take orange juice concentrate out of freezer to thaw.
2. Put the juice, soda, honey, water, and ice cubes into large bowl and mix well with spoon.
3. Serve cold.

Q. Why is Shavuot called the Holiday of Weeks?

A. Because we count seven full weeks from Pesach to Shavuot in anticipation of receiving the Torah.

Q. What are 3 additional names for Shavuot?

A. Chag HaKatzir -- The Festival of the Harvest
Yom HaBikkurim -- The Day of the First Fruits
Atzeret -- The Conclusion

10 Karat cake

Ingredients

5-6 medium carrots
1 cup brown sugar
2 eggs
3/4 cup oil
1-1/4 cups flour
1/2 teaspoon baking soda
1 teaspoon baking powder
1/2 teaspoon vanilla
1 teaspoon vanilla
1/2 cup chopped nuts
1 tablespoon lemon juice

Utensils

measuring cups
measuring spoons
potato peeler
coarse grater
bowl
wooden spoon
tube pan

How To Do It

1. Peel and grate carrots. Measure 1 cup of grated carrots. Put carrots into bowl.
2. Add remaining ingredients to bowl. Mix well with wooden spoon.
3. Pour cake mixture into pan.
4. Bake at 350 degrees Fahrenheit for 40 minutes.

Oven Temperature Chart

FAHRENHEIT ❄ ❄ ❄ CENTRIGRADE

200	❄	❄	❄	❄	❄	100
225	❄	❄	❄	❄	❄	110
250	❄	❄	❄	❄	❄	130
275	❄	❄	❄	❄	❄	140
300	❄	❄	❄	❄	❄	150
325	❄	❄	❄	❄	❄	170
350	❄	❄	❄	❄	❄	180
375	❄	❄	❄	❄	❄	190
400	❄	❄	❄	❄	❄	200
425	❄	❄	❄	❄	❄	220
450	❄	❄	❄	❄	❄	230
475	❄	❄	❄	❄	❄	240

MEASURES

3 tsps. = 1 Tbsp. = 30 g = 15 milliliters
4 Tblsp. = 1/4 cup = 60 g. = 2 ounces
5 Tblsp.
& 1 tsp. = 1/3 cup
1/2 cup = 120 g = 4 ounces
3/4 cup = 180 g = 6 ounces
1 cup = 250 g = 8 ounces

WEIGHTS

1/2	ounce	=	15	grams
1	ounce	=	30	grams
1-3/4	ounce	=	50	grams
2-1/2	ounces	=	75	grams
3-1/2	ounces	=	100	grams
4	ounces	=	125	grams
8	ounces	=	250	grams
17	ounces	=	500	grams
35	ounces	=	1000	grams

INDEX